Wayne + Lolita
Hayworth
10-06

Epic Battles
of the Last Days

RICK JOYNER

MorningStar Publications
A DIVISION OF MORNINGSTAR FELLOWSHIP CHURCH
375 Star Light Drive, Fort Mill, SC 29715

Epic Battles of the Last Days
by Rick Joyner
Copyright © 1995
Mass Market Edition, 2006

Distributed by MorningStar Publications, Inc.,
a division of MorningStar Fellowship Church
375 Star Light Drive, Fort Mill, SC 29715

International Standard Book Number: 1-929371-77-2

Cover Design: Kevin Lepp
Book Layout: Dana Zondory

MorningStar's website: www.morningstarministries.org
For information call 1-800-542-0278.

TABLE OF CONTENTS

Introduction 5

PART I
THE BIG PICTURE • 17

Chapter One
The Two Ministries 19

Chapter Two
Racism and the Spirit of Death 43

PART II
The Stronghold of Witchcraft • 73

Chapter Three
Overcoming Witchcraft 75

Chapter Four
The Stinger 89

Chapter Five
Combating New Age Witchcraft 105

Chapter Six
The Stronghold of Illegitimate Authority 121

PART III
The Religious Spirit • 135

Chapter Seven
Combating the Religious Spirit 137

Chapter Eight
The Spirit of Jezebel 157

Chapter Nine
The Warning Signs of the Religious Spirit 171

PART IV
The Gates of Hell
and the Doors of Heaven • 179

Chapter Ten
Understanding Spiritual Gates 181

Chapter Eleven
When Heaven and Hell Collide 197

Chapter Twelve
The Two Mandates 213

Chapter Thirteen
The Battle for Life and Liberty 229

Chapter Fourteen
Twelve Lessons on Warfare 245

Introduction

The Lord gave dominion over the earth to the first man, Adam. When Adam sinned, he became the slave of sin, and all that was under his domain was subjected to bondage with him. It was for this reason that the Lord Jesus referred to Himself as the **"Son of man,"** and the Apostle Paul referred to Him as **"the last Adam"** (**see I Corinthians 15:45**). A man was given dominion over the earth, a man lost it, and a man had to recover it. That man who recovered it was Jesus, who fully conquered sin on the cross and recovered dominion over the earth. At that time, He was given the authority to reclaim the world and establish His kingdom of righteousness. Why did He not do it then?

As a wise friend, Paul Cain, once said to me, "Most heresies are the result of men trying to carry to logical conclusions that which God has only revealed in part." Even a cursory look at church history reveals the truth

5

of that insight. There seems to be a special trap set for those who have tried to answer the question of why Jesus didn't immediately assume His rightful kingship over the whole earth. Therefore, I will endeavor to be especially careful not to go beyond what has been clearly revealed in the Scriptures on this subject. Even so, the Bible says a great deal about this matter which is of supreme importance in these times, yet is seldom addressed in the mainstream of Christianity.

The messianic prophecies speak of both a suffering Servant and a conquering King. The Lamb has come, and the King is yet to come. If Jesus is to be a conquering King, He must have something left to conquer. We can presume that evil will not be fully conquered until He returns. It is just as obvious that the church is here both to preach the kingdom and to boldly confront the strongholds of the enemy. We are to be the **"salt of the earth,"** and **"the light of the world" (see Matthew 5:13-14).** If corruption and darkness are spreading, it must be because the church has not been doing what she has been called to do. This must be the case as the enemy has been successful in blurring much of our basic mandate on this earth.

The Son of God appeared for this purpose, that He might destroy the works of the devil (I John 3:8).

Because **"appeared"** is past tense, this Scripture is clearly not talking about His second coming, but His first. Though the Lord came to redeem a people for

Himself, He did not come just for that purpose, but also to destroy the works of the devil. A major part of His plan for destroying the works of the devil is to do it through the church, as He confirmed in John 17:18:

As Thou [Father] didst send Me into the world, I also have sent them into the world.

Just as He came to destroy the works of the devil, He has sent the church with that same purpose. If this is a purpose for which we have been sent, one way that we could measure the success of our calling would be to count the works of the evil one that we have been used to destroy. Paul addressed this in his exhortation in II Corinthians 10:3-6:

For though we walk in the flesh, we do not war according to the flesh,

for the weapons of our warfare are not of the flesh, but divinely powerful for the destruction of fortresses.

We are destroying speculations and every lofty thing raised up against the knowledge of God, and we are taking every thought captive to the obedience of Christ,

and we are ready to punish all disobedience, whenever your obedience is complete.

If we are using the weapons of our warfare properly, we should be able to point to enemy fortresses that have been destroyed. **"Every lofty thing**

raised up against the knowledge of God" should be falling before us. Is there any congregation that has walked, or is walking, in this? If not, why?

The purpose of this book is to address this question, illuminating some of the most powerful and deadly evil strongholds of these last days and focusing on the biblical truths that will destroy them. This will release the knowledge of God and bring men into obedience to His Christ, as Paul declared (see II Corinthians 10:5). Whether or not we believe in a pre-tribulation rapture is not the issue. Regardless of when we are caught up to be with the Lord, we must be found fighting against the strongholds of the enemy, and destroying his fortresses.

The Lord Jesus had both the authority and the power to subdue evil and take dominion over the earth after His resurrection. He could do it right now by simply declaring it—the power of a single word from Him is more than enough to destroy all of the works of the enemy. Obviously He must have a good reason for letting us do it instead.

Who Are We?

There are several metaphors used to describe the church. We are a "bride," a "body," a "holy nation," "God's field," "sheep," "a kingdom of priests," and "soldiers." Some of these designations may seem to conflict with others, but they don't, as long as we understand the principle of timing. There is a time for the church to be a family, and there is a time to be an army. It takes wisdom and sensitivity to the Spirit to know when to give ourselves to each. If we do not have this sensitivity, we will run the risk of being either irrelevant to the times or in grave danger ourselves.

Our first calling is to fellowship with God. Our first and greatest loss from the Fall was our intimacy with Him. The very first thing that is meant to be restored by redemption is our intimacy with God. If there is any way that we can measure true Christian maturity, or the degree to which redemption has worked in our lives, it would be by how close we are to Him.

We will never win a single battle by our own wisdom or strength; it will only be by the power of the One who dwells within us. Therefore, the chief strategy of spiritual warfare is to get closer to the King and walk in greater obedience to Him. The degree to which we walk in true spiritual authority is determined by the degree to which the King lives within us. The kingdom only comes with the presence of the King. Our first calling is to be a family and to know Him as our Father, which does not negate our calling to also be an army and know Him as our King. There is a time for covered dish dinners, and there is a time to put on the whole armor of God and march out into the fray. Wisdom is knowing when to do each.

Our Finest Hour

The church is at war. This war will not end because we do not like it, or do not want to fight.

Fortresses of darkness are being raised up on every front. Evil strongholds are being erected in the minds and hearts of people at an unprecedented rate in government, education, business, entertainment, neighborhoods, and even in the church. This is happening on our watch!

The church is now being pressed on every side, and it seems that she is in retreat in every way. Even so, as improbable as it may seem at this time, we have the enemy surrounded! The church is about to win her greatest victory. This is her finest hour—the retreat is over and the advance is about to begin.

From the beginning, virtually all the prophets prophesied of the great battle of the last days, and they all longed to more fully understand what they were only seeing **"through a glass, darkly"** (see **I Corinthians 13:12 KJV**). We have now come to a generation that will do more than just speak prophetically of the times—this generation has been called to carry the banner of the Lord into the greatest epic battle of all time. The last day church has been given one of the greatest privileges that has ever been bestowed by God—to be on the field of battle for the ultimate confrontation between light and darkness.

The **"great cloud of witnesses"** (see **Hebrews 12:1 NIV),** composed of righteous men and women from every age, is now watching the church. They have earned this right. They will be cheering us on as we embrace the cross and carry it forward against the hordes of darkness. The Lord has already defeated our enemies. He could have banished them to hell on the day of His resurrection, but He left them here for us because He wants His bride to share the honor! In these last days she will surely be **"as awesome as an army with banners" (see Song of Solomon 6:10).**

The Lord has called His bride to rule and reign with Him as joint heir. He has let this conflict continue for more than 2,000 years so that His bride could prove herself, as well as grow in the faithfulness and grace needed for her great position. In the intensity of battle, when life and death can hang on every decision, not only is the true nature of a person revealed, but, as Paul explained, **"each man's work will become evident; for the day will show it because it is to be revealed with fire, and the fire itself will test the quality of each man's work" (I Corinthians 3:13).**

The whole creation, including the principalities and powers, is watching to see what the church is really made of. Will we love the Lord, truth, and righteousness more than we love this present world? Only those who **"did not love their life even to death"** are fit for the great throne that has been prepared for the bride of Christ (see Revelation 12:11).

This book is but one trumpet call among many that are now summoning the saints to battle. The enemy is already being engaged on every front and on the walls of every fortress. This is a call to further mobilize the church to battle against some of the greatest strongholds of our time. This time of great darkness is our greatest opportunity. Now the enemy is being fully revealed, but this is so that we can destroy his works. He who is in us is much greater than he who is in the world (see I John 4:4), and those who carry the banner of His truth need never retreat before the hordes of darkness.

This Is Personal

This is not a self-help manual; it is not intended to address personal problems. We are reaching for something higher. However, the issues that are addressed in this book can potentially have a profound impact on our lives in almost every way.

We must heal the "walking wounded" and get them back to the front! For many, the healing will come as soon as they get their attention off of themselves and onto the real battle. We do not have time to keep navel-gazing, drowning in our own self-centeredness! Every human in this world has been wounded. We all have been taken advantage of, betrayed, abused, and assaulted. Certainly more of the same is coming our way, which the Lord made clear when He said, **"In the world you have tribulation..." (John 16:33)**. We do not have time to keep feeling sorry for ourselves—it is time to rise up and destroy the works of the one who is behind it all.

Self-pity will keep us defeated. Forgiveness, which is rooted in self-sacrifice, will enable us to withstand the unjustified attacks, and keep getting up and coming back just like the apostles of old. There is an opportunity for a much greater victory than we ever dreamed. We must get over the petty, selfish cares of this world that have kept us so entangled. Self-centeredness is the root of all the evil that has come into this world, and we will not be able to drive it out as long as it prevails in our own camp.

This is not to imply that many do not have genuine problems that need attention and help. Even so, most of the problems that presently consume the church would take care of themselves if we simply gave our attention to the Lord's business. As He promised,

> "For this reason I say to you, do not be anxious for your life, as to what you shall eat, or what you shall drink; nor for your body, as to what you shall put on. Is not life more than food, and the body than clothing?
>
> "Look at the birds of the air, that they do not sow, neither do they reap, nor gather into barns, and yet your heavenly Father feeds them. Are you not worth much more than they?" (Matthew 6:25-26)
>
> "But seek first His kingdom and His righteousness; and all these things shall be added to you.
>
> "Therefore do not be anxious for tomorrow; for tomorrow will care for itself.

**Each day has enough trouble of its own"
(Matthew 6:33-34).**

Misunderstandings and persecutions can provide our greatest opportunities to learn the forgiveness that leads to Christlikeness. These are the source of some of our greatest blessings, as the Lord declared:

"Blessed are those who have been persecuted for the sake of righteousness, for theirs is the kingdom of heaven.

"Blessed are you when men cast insults at you, and persecute you, and say all kinds of evil against you falsely, on account of Me.

**"Rejoice, and be glad, for your reward in heaven is great, for so they persecuted the prophets who were before you"
(Matthew 5:10-12).**

Do not worry—there will be plenty of these blessings for all of us! And they are being used to separate those who live for themselves from those who love truth and righteousness. The Scriptures are clear: By the end, the camp of the Lord will be free of both cowards and traitors.

The strongholds addressed in this book are not the only ones we face, but they are some of the deadliest ones the church will confront in these last days. No individual or church can confront every stronghold, but we must first recognize the ones in our own camp and drive them out. While one church mobilizes to battle a specific stronghold, the congregation next door may mobilize to attack a different one.

However, we must always remember that we are all on the same side. It is not unnatural for us to think the battle we are facing is the most important one, and it will be the most important for us. But let us always respect the different callings and purposes given to the different congregations and movements in the body of Christ. Let us not forget who the real enemy is.

For our struggle is not against flesh and blood, but against the rulers, against the powers, against the world forces of this darkness, against the spiritual forces of wickedness in the heavenly places (Ephesians 6:12).

Above all, we must fight to win. This is not a game, even though the ultimate victory is already decided. The Lord carries the responsibility for the universe on His shoulders, but He has given us, as His bride, the responsibility for many souls. When He returns, may we present to Him the reward worthy of His sacrifice—multitudes from every tongue, nation, and tribe, dressed in white robes without spot or blemish, passionately in love with Him.

Part I
THE BIG PICTURE

Chapter One

The Two Ministries

The Scriptures reveal that there are two acts which go on continually before the throne of God—intercession and accusation. The conflict between these two is a focal point of the battle between the kingdom of God and the kingdom of darkness. Because God has chosen to make the church His dwelling place, and therefore the place of His throne, it is in the heart of the church that this battle now rages.

Jesus **"always lives to make intercession" (see Hebrews 7:25).** His fundamental nature is to be an intercessor, a priest. To the degree that we abide in Him, Jesus will use us to intercede. For this reason, His church is called to be a **"house of prayer for all the nations" (see Mark 11:17).**

Satan is called **"the accuser of our brethren... who accuses them before our God day and night" (Revelation 12:10).** To the degree that the enemy has access to our lives, he will use us to accuse and criticize the brethren. Like the two trees in the Garden of Eden, we must all choose which of these ministries we are going to partake of.

We may ask how Satan could continue to accuse the saints before God if he has been thrown out of heaven and no longer has access to the throne. The answer is that Satan uses the saints, who do have access to the throne, to do this diabolical work for him.

Satan's Greatest Victory

Satan is called by many titles, but certainly his most effective guise has been **"the accuser of our brethren" (see Revelation 12:10).** This title was given to him because of his effectiveness in getting brother to turn against brother. From the time that he entered the Garden to thwart the purpose of man, this has been his specialty. Even when there were just two brothers on earth, they could not get along (see Genesis 4). The presence of Satan will always promote discord and division.

Satan's greatest victory over the church is in turning the brethren against each other. Accusation has been his most effective and deadly tool in destroying the light, the power, and the witness of the body of Christ. Our ability to accomplish our purpose in this world will be determined by the degree to which we can dispel our deadly enemy and learn to live for one another.

The greatest threat to Satan's domain is the unity of the church. The devil knows very well the awesome authority that Jesus has given to any two believers who will agree. He knows that with agreement between just two saints, the Father will give them what they ask. He understands that one saint can put a thousand to flight, but two of them together can put ten thousand to flight (see Deuteronomy 32:30). Unity does not just increase our spiritual authority—it multiplies it. Unfortunately, the enemy has understood all of this much better than the church has.

The access which the accuser has to most believers is through their insecurity. This drives them to become territorial or possessive. The insecure are threatened by anything that they cannot control. The accuser may use many seemingly noble justifications for a believer's attacks on others, such as to protect the truth or the sheep, but rarely is there a division in the church that is not rooted in self-preservation or a clinging to territory.

The greater the authority or influence that people have in the church, the bigger the target they make. Satan knows well that if he can make a leader territorial or self-centered, the leader will in turn sow these same tendencies in all of those under him, making the division or sectarian spirit all the more destructive.

Ironically, the resulting division that is caused by trying to protect our domains is the very thing that cuts us off from true spiritual authority and anointing. This ultimately results in our losing the very thing we are so desperately trying to preserve, which is an incontrovertible law of the spirit: **"For whoever wishes to save his life shall lose it; but whoever loses his life for My sake shall find it" (Matthew 16:25).** Isaiah also addressed this issue:

> **"Then your light will break out like the dawn, and your recovery will speedily spring forth; and your righteousness will go before you; and the glory of the LORD will be your rear guard.**
>
> **"Then you will call, and the LORD will answer; you will cry, and He will say, 'Here I am.' If you remove the yoke from your midst, the pointing of the finger, and speaking wickedness" (Isaiah 58:8-9).**

Here we are promised that if we remove the yoke of criticism from our midst (which is portrayed as **"the pointing of the finger, and speaking wickedness"**), our light will break out, our healing will come speedily, the glory of the Lord will follow us, and He will answer our prayers. It is likely that nothing would so radically change the church, and the lives of individual believers, more than having our criticisms changed into intercession. Likewise, it is probable that an addiction to criticism is the main reason why there is so little light, so little healing, so little of the glory of the Lord, and so little answered prayer in the church today.

Criticism Is Pride

Criticism is one of the ultimate manifestations of pride, because whenever we criticize someone else, we are assuming that we are superior to them. Pride brings that which any rational human should fear the most—God's resistance. **"God resists the proud, but gives grace to the humble" (James 4:6 NKJV).** We would be better off having all the demons in hell resisting us than God!

Pride caused the first Fall, and it has been a root in probably every fall from grace since. Peter's betrayal of the Lord is one of the great examples of how pride causes us to fall from grace. On that same night when Peter betrayed the Lord, he had earlier charged a Roman cohort to defend his Lord. Even though this was misguided zeal, it was impressive courage—a Roman cohort was composed of eight hundred men!

When the Lord warned Peter of his impending denial of Him, Peter challenged the Son of God, declaring in effect, "They may all fall away from you, but not me." Peter knew that he was a man of courage and would be willing to even die for the Lord; he just did not know where the courage came from. The Lord did not cause Peter to fall that night; He just removed the grace by which he was standing. Then the fearless man who had charged a Roman cohort could not even stand before a servant girl! (see Luke 22:54-62)

None of us can stand, except by the grace of God. This is more than a cliché; it is a basic biblical truth. When we condemn others who are having problems, we are putting ourselves in jeopardy of falling into the same sins. That is why Paul warned us:

Brethren, even if a man is caught in any trespass, you who are spiritual, restore such a one in a spirit of gentleness; each one looking to yourself, lest you too be tempted (Galatians 6:1).

Who Are We Criticizing?

When we criticize another Christian, we are actually saying that God's workmanship does not meet up to our standards—that we could do it better. When we criticize someone else's children, who will take offense? The parents! This is no less true with God. When we judge one of His people, we are judging Him. When we judge one of His leaders, we are really judging His leadership. We are saying, in effect, that He does not know what He is doing with the leadership He is providing.

Such grumbling and complaining is the same problem that kept the first generation of the children of Israel from possessing their promised land. Their grumbling caused them to spend their entire lives wandering in dry places, and this is the chief reason why so many Christians do not walk in the promises of God. We have been warned:

Do not speak against one another, brethren. He who speaks against a brother, or judges his brother, speaks against the law, and judges the law; but if you judge the law, you are not a doer of the law, but a judge of it.

> **There is only one Lawgiver and Judge, the One who is able to save and to destroy; but who are you who judge your neighbor? (James 4:11-12)**

When we judge our brother, we are judging the law, which is the same as judging the Lawgiver. Also, when we "point the finger" to criticize others, we are asking for a stricter judgment on ourselves:

> **"Judge not, that you be not judged.**
>
> **"For with what judgment you judge, you will be judged; and with the measure you use, it will be measured back to you"** (Matthew 7:1-2 NKJV).

The Spirit of Poverty

I once visited a state that was under one of the most powerful spirits of poverty that I have witnessed in this country. This was remarkable because it was a state of great beauty and natural resources, with talented and resourceful people. However, another characteristic of the people there also stood out— they seemed to inevitably scorn and criticize the prosperous or powerful.

Almost all the churches in this state were very small, and my conversations with pastors there would inevitably turn to criticizing "mega churches" and "mega ministries," which these pastors told me were the source of their problems. This situation was even sadder because many of these small church pastors were much more anointed and were called to walk in more spiritual authority than the leaders of these mega churches or ministries that they criticized. Yet their judgments had restrained the grace of God in their lives.

It is biblical that we may sometimes need to be abased and sometimes we need to abound. The Apostle Paul even claimed to have gone hungry at times, and he sternly warned us to be content if we just have food and covering (see I Timothy 6:8). However, if I am to be abased, I want to do it in submission to God and to what He is trying to work in my life, not in submission to an evil spirit of poverty. I certainly do not want to be yoked to poverty because of my own evil judgment of others.

Many pastors yoke themselves and their congregations to financial poverty by criticizing how other men of God take up offerings. Because of their judgments, they cannot even take up a biblical offering without feeling guilty. As Isaiah 58 implies, the primary reason for the darkness, lack of healing, unanswered prayer, and lack of the glory of God is our own critical spirit. Over the years I have met many people who have had exceptional mantles of spiritual authority but little spiritual fruit, and this critical attitude has nearly always been a prevailing characteristic in their lives. They had judged and criticized the ministries of others who were gaining influence, and had thereby disqualified themselves from the grace of God in that area. Our criticisms will bring us to poverty. **"Death and life are in the power of the tongue, and those who love it will eat its fruit" (Proverbs 18:21).**

As Solomon observed: **"But the path of the just is like the shining sun, that shines ever brighter unto the perfect day. The way of the wicked is like darkness; they do not know what makes them stumble" (Proverbs 4:18-19 NKJV).** If we are walking in righteousness, we will be walking in increasing light. Those who stumble around in the dark seldom know the reason for that darkness, or they would not be in it. However, the critical person is usually critical of everyone but himself, and therefore he cannot see his own problems. As the Lord stated, he is so busy looking for specks in the eyes of his brothers that he cannot see the big log in his own eye, which is the reason for his blindness (see Matthew 7:35).

Stumbling Blocks

The Lord indicated that the very last thing that we should ever want to be is a stumbling block. He said that it would be better for us not to have been born than to cause even one of His little ones to stumble (see Matthew 18:6-7).

In the same conversation in which He warned us not to become a stumbling block, He gave clear instructions about how we are to deal with a brother who is in sin. First, we must go to the person in private. Only after he has rejected our counsel do we go to him with another brother. Then, only after he has rejected both should we ever go before the rest of the church with the issue. If we do not follow this pattern, we will be in jeopardy of suffering a fate worse than the person who is in sin—we will become a stumbling block (see Matthew 18:15-17).

This tendency toward unrighteous judgment in the church is very possibly why many will come before the Lord on the judgment day having done many great things in His name, but will still hear those terrible words: **"...depart from Me, you who practice lawlessness" (Matthew 7:23).** By the Lord's own teachings it would be very hard for us to overstate the importance of this terrible sin of unrighteous judgment.

I have heard numerous excuses for not following the Matthew 18 pattern for dealing with sin. People will say, "I knew they would not listen to me" or "If they have a public ministry, we have a right to expose them publicly." However, the Lord did not say that we only had to comply with His instructions when we knew that the people would listen to us. He clearly implied that some will not hear which is why there are the subsequent steps.

As far as the "public ministry" excuse goes, this, too, is flawed logic, because every ministry is public, at least to some degree. Who determines the point at which the ministry has become so public that it frees us from compliance with God's Word? The Lord gave no such conditions. Those who take such liberties with the clear commandments given by Jesus Himself are by this logic claiming to have authority to add to the Word of God.

If we believe someone with a large ministry is in sin, and we are unable to confront him with our discernment, then we must not be the one to bring the judgment. Do not accuse—intercede! The Lord is able to judge His own house, and He is able to make a way for us if we are the ones He wants to use. If He does not make a way for us, we must trust Him to do the correcting in His own time and His own way. Again, this is to protect us from coming under a judgment that is even more severe than the brother who is in sin.

If we have not followed the Lord's prescribed manner for dealing with a brother who is in sin, we have absolutely no right to talk about it to anyone else, much less go public with it. It should not even be shared in order to get another's opinion on the matter. What we may call getting someone else's opinion, God usually calls gossip. He is not fooled, and we will pay the price for such indiscretions. Even if we follow all of the steps in Matthew 18, and determine that we must bring an issue before the church, our goal must always be to save the brother from his sin, not just to expose him.

Love Covers Sin

Let us be careful not to become petty with our challenges to the presumed sin in another Christian's life. **"Love covers a multitude of sins"** (see **I Peter**

4:8). The majority of us still have a few hundred things wrong with us, and the Lord is usually only dealing with one or two at a time because that is all we can take. It is one of Satan's strategies to try and distract us into dealing with the other two hundred problems simultaneously, resulting in frustration and defeat. Matthew 18 was not given to us to use as a club for beating up on each other or even for letting a brother know how he offended us. If we have love, we will cover most of those sins, unless they are bringing unnecessary injury to our brother. We must use this Scripture, and indeed all Scriptures, in love, not out of self-preservation or retaliation.

Of course, the Lord Jesus Himself is our perfect model. When He corrected the seven churches in Revelation, He gave us an example for bringing correction in the church. He first praised each church and highlighted what they were doing right. He then straightforwardly addressed their problems. Incredibly, He even gave Jezebel time to repent! (see Revelation 2:20-21) He then gave each church a wonderful promise of reward for overcoming their problems. The Lord never changes. When He brings correction today, it always comes wrapped in encouragement, hope, and promises.

The "accuser of the brethren" is also trying to bring correction to the church. However, his methods and goals are obviously quite different. Jesus encourages and gives hope; Satan condemns and tries to impart hopelessness. Jesus builds us up so that we can handle the correction; Satan tears us down, trying to get us to quit. Jesus loves us and wants to lift us up; Satan's goal is always our destruction.

Discernment

Criticism can be rooted in true discernment. Those we criticize may well be in error. The pastors mentioned previously, who criticized the manipulative ways others raised money, were accurate in their discernment. We must walk in discernment, as Paul declared, **"Do you not judge those who are within the church?"** (**I Corinthians 5:12**) The issue is how we deal with what we discern—are we going to use it to accuse or to intercede? How we deal with discernment can determine the outcome of our own spiritual lives.

> **A worthless person, a wicked man, walks with a perverse mouth;**
>
> **he winks with his eyes, he shuffles his feet, he points with his fingers;**
>
> **Perversity is in his heart, he devises evil continually, he sows discord.**
>
> **Therefore his calamity shall come suddenly; suddenly he shall be broken without remedy (Proverbs 6:12-15 NKJV).**

Much of what has been paraded as discernment is nothing more than suspicion—a spiritual disguise used to mask territorial preservation. Even without the spiritual gift of discernment, James gave us clear guidelines for discerning the source of wisdom, which, if the church had heeded in the past, would have kept us from some of our most humiliating failures:

> **Who is wise and understanding among you? Let him show by good conduct that his works are done in the meekness of wisdom.**
>
> **But if you have bitter envy and self-seeking in your hearts, do not boast and lie against the truth.**
>
> **This wisdom does not descend from above, but is earthly, sensual, demonic.**
>
> **For where envy and self-seeking exist, confusion and every evil thing are there.**
>
> **But the wisdom that is from above is first pure, then peaceable, gentle, willing to yield, full of mercy and good fruits, without partiality and without hypocrisy.**
>
> **Now the fruit of righteousness is sown in peace by those who make peace (James 3:13-18 NKJV).**

We are saved by grace, and we will need all the grace we can get in order to make it through this life. But if we want to receive grace, we had better learn to give grace, because we are going to reap what we sow. If we expect to receive mercy, we must start sowing mercy, and most of us are going to need all the mercy we can get. The very last thing that we want to do is come before the Lord on the Day of Judgment with our brother's blood on our hands, just as He warned:

"You have heard that it was said to those of old, 'You shall not murder, and whoever murders will be in danger of the judgment.'

"But I say to you that whoever is angry with his brother without a cause shall be in danger of the judgment. And whoever says to his brother, 'Raca!' [empty head] shall be in danger of the council. But whoever says, 'You fool!' shall be in danger of hell fire.

"Therefore if you bring your gift to the altar, and there remember that your brother has something against you,

leave your gift there before the altar, and go your way. First be reconciled to your brother, and then come and offer your gift.

"Agree with your adversary quickly, while you are on the way with him, lest your adversary deliver you to the judge, the judge hand you over to the officer, and you be thrown into prison [bondage].

"Assuredly, I say to you, you will by no means get out of there till you have paid the last penny" (Matthew 5:21-26 NKJV).

It is clear by this warning that, if we have been guilty of slandering a brother, we should forget about our offerings to the Lord until we have been reconciled to our brother. He linked these together because we often think that our sacrifices and offerings can compensate for such sins, but they never will. We will stay in the prisons we make for ourselves with our judgments until we either have "paid the last penny" or until we are reconciled to the brother we slandered.

The Lord said that when He returned He was going to judge between the sheep and the goats (see Matthew 25:31-46). Those who are judged sheep will inherit the kingdom and eternal life. Those who are designated goats will be sent to eternal judgment. The separation will be determined by how each group has treated the Lord, which will be determined by how they have treated His people. John pointed out this same principle:

> **If someone says, "I love God," and hates his brother, he is a liar; for the one who does not love his brother whom he has seen, cannot love God whom he has not seen (I John 4:20).**

> **Everyone who hates his brother is a murderer; and you know that no murderer has eternal life abiding in him.**

> **We know love by this, that He laid down His life for us; and we ought to lay down our lives for the brethren (I John 3:15-16).**

If we really have Christ's Spirit, then we will also have His nature. How many of us, knowing that our best friends were about to desert us and even deny that they knew us, would have "earnestly desired" to have one last meal with them? (see Luke 22:15) Our Lord's love for His disciples was never conditional on their doing right. Even though He knew they were about to desert Him and deny Him, He loved them to the end—He even gave His life for them. When He saw our sin He did not criticize us; He laid down His life for us. He has commanded us to love with that same love.

War Between Spiritual Generations

One of the great tragedies of church history has been the way leaders of each move of God have become opposers and persecutors of subsequent moves. To date, this trend has not failed. The Lord uses this to help purify and work humility into those He is about to release with increasing power and authority, but this is still a great tragedy. Numerous leaders have spent their lives serving faithfully only to finish as vessels for the accuser who makes them a stumbling block for the next move.

What is it that causes leaders of one move to become opposers of the next move? There are several factors involved, which we must understand and be delivered of or we will end up doing the same thing. We may think and say that we would never do such a thing, but that is what everyone has thought and said who ended up doing it. **"Therefore let him who thinks he stands take heed lest he fall" (I Corinthians 10:12).** The pride that causes us to assume we would never sin in a certain way is one of the very factors that often leads to doing it.

This problem actually precedes church history and goes all the way back to the very first two brothers born into this world. John observed why the older could not stand the younger:

> **For this is the message which you have heard from the beginning, that we should love one another;**
>
> **not as Cain, who was of the evil one, and slew his brother. And for what reason did he slay him? Because his deeds were evil, and his brother's were righteous (I John 3:11-12).**

Each new move of the Holy Spirit has resulted in the restoration of more light to the church. This light is not actually "new truth," but truth that was lost by the church through the dark ages of her history. Regardless of what we call our opposition to new moves of God, a basic reason for most of it is jealousy. Those in leadership who have often been faithful to the light they have had for a time, have difficulty believing that the Lord would want to use anyone but them for further restoration of His truth and purposes.

The only remedy leaders have to keep them from ultimately falling into this terrible trap is to seek the humility and nature of John the Baptist. This man is one of the greatest examples of true spiritual ministry. His whole purpose in life was to prepare the Lord's way and point to Him, then to decrease as the greater One increased. It was John's joy to see the One who followed him going further than he went.

The Foundation of True Ministry

True spiritual leaders must become "spiritual eunuchs." A eunuch's whole purpose was to prepare the bride for the king. It was not even possible for the eunuch to desire the bride, but his whole joy was in his king's joy. When we use the ministry in order to build our own reputation or find those who will serve us, we will not be operating in the authority of Christ. Paul exhorted us:

> **Do nothing from selfishness or empty conceit, but with humility of mind let each of you regard one another as more important than himself;**

> **do not merely look out for your own personal interests, but also for the interests of others.**

> **Have this attitude in yourselves which was also in Christ Jesus,**

> **who, although He existed in the form of God, did not regard equality with God a thing to be grasped,**

> **but emptied Himself, taking the form of a bond-servant, and being made in the likeness of men.**

**And being found in appearance as a man,
He humbled Himself by becoming obedient
to the point of death, even death on a cross.**

**Therefore also God highly exalted Him,
and bestowed on Him the name which is
above every name (Philippians 2:3-9).**

This is the pattern that Jesus set for everyone
who would follow Him in leadership. Humility comes
before authority and position. He said in Luke 14:11:
**"For everyone who exalts himself shall be humbled,
and he who humbles himself shall be exalted."** A key
word here is **"everyone."** James added, **"Humble
yourselves in the presence of the Lord, and He will
exalt you" (James 4:10).** Peter stated: **"Humble yourselves, therefore, under the mighty hand of God, that
He may exalt you at the proper time" (I Peter 5:6).**

In all of these texts we see that it is our job to
humble ourselves and it is the Lord's job to do the
exalting. It is clear that if we try to do His job, He will
do our job, and He can do either one of them much
better than we can. The evil spirits of self-promotion
and territorial preservation have done much damage
to the church. They have caused many potentially
great leaders to be disqualified from receiving further
anointing and authority. The influence that we gain
by our own self-promotion or manipulation will be a
stumbling block that keeps us from attaining positions
that God would otherwise give us.

It has not always been the older generation of
leaders that is the stumbling block for the new. The

new generation can be just as guilty of causing the previous one to stumble! The very arrogance of presuming that we are the new "cutting edge" generation of God's purposes reveals a pride that God has to resist. This attitude is a humiliating slap in the face to men and women who have given their lives to faithfully serving the Lord and His people for years.

Jesus did not ridicule John the Baptist for being a part of the old order—He honored him. Jesus even submitted Himself to John's ministry. This submission did not mean that He allowed John to control Him, but He acknowledged John's vital role, esteeming both him and his work.

Later, when Jesus was asked the source of His authority, he pointed to John and asked His inquisitors if they knew the source of John's baptism. The answer to that question was the answer to their question (see Matthew 21:23-27). John was the last of an order; he was there to represent all of those who had prophesied of the coming Messiah from the very beginning. John was their representative to acknowledge Jesus as the One of whom they had all spoken, the very Lamb of God. Jesus acknowledged the validity of John's ministry as one of the credentials of His own authority.

Likewise, in order to **"fulfill all righteousness" (see Matthew 3:15),** those who are of the new generation must submit to the ministries of all those who have gone before them. We are presently in the midst of seeing a new spiritual generation emerge. It is also

for a time

apparent that the previous movements are beginning to decrease as the new order increases. However, it is crucial that the leaders of the new order honor those who went before them, or they will be in jeopardy of disqualifying themselves from going further. The arrogance of the new order can be just as much an affront to the Spirit of God as that of the old who start to resist God in the new things He is beginning to do.

Why the Abused Become Abusers

Why is it that abused children grow up to be abusers? Why is it that accused saints grow up to be accusers? The answer is the same for both questions. Abused children usually grow up determined not to be like their parents, so they become reactionary. This does not lead to grace, but can actually nurture bitterness, which ultimately results in their becoming just like their parents. Only humility and forgiveness will break that cycle. The sins of the parents will become the sins of the children until we receive the grace of the cross. Because God gives His grace to the humble, we must understand that without His help we will take on the sins of our parents. That is one reason why many of the great leaders in Scripture prayed to be forgiven for the sins of their fathers.

Elijah Must Come

There will be a spiritual generation that will be persecuted like every generation has before it, but which will not go on to persecute the next generation.

This movement will not become subject to the "pride of generations," assuming that all things will be concluded with them. Those of this generation will have found the grace of the cross and will have forgiven, from the heart, those who mistreated them.

This coming generation will also have vision that their children, both spiritual and natural, may go further in Christ than they did, and they will rejoice in it. They will give their lives to making the way of the next generation as smooth as possible, and then they will happily decrease as that generation arises. This will be the generation of the spirit of Elijah, who will return the hearts of the fathers to the sons, and the hearts of the sons to the fathers (see Malachi 4:6).

Our ability to be the generation that prepares the way for the Lord and His ultimate purposes will be determined by which of the two ministries we become a part of—accusation or intercession. Let us now remove the terrible yoke of "pointing the finger" from our midst and begin turning our criticisms into intercession.

"Then your light will break out like the dawn, and your recovery will speedily spring forth; and your righteousness will go before you; the glory of the Lord will be your rear guard.

"Then you will call, and the Lord will answer; you will cry, and He will say, 'Here I am.'

"And the Lord will continually guide you, and satisfy your desire in scorched places, and give strength to your bones; and you will be like a watered garden, and like a spring of water whose waters do not fail.

"And those from among you will rebuild the ancient ruins; and you will raise up the age-old foundations; and you will be called the repairer of the breach, the restorer of the streets in which to dwell" (Isaiah 58:8-9, 11-12).

Chapter Two

Racism and the Spirit of Death

> "For nation will rise against nation, and kingdom against kingdom, and in various places there will be famines and earthquakes.
>
> "But all these things are merely the beginning of birth pangs" (Matthew 24:7-8).

The word that is translated **"nation"** in this text is the Greek word *ethnos*, from which we derive our English word "ethnic." Jesus' discourse in Matthew 24 was given in response to a question about the signs of the end of the age. He declared that a prominent sign would be ethnic conflict. In fulfillment of this prediction, one of the greatest issues now facing the world and the church is ethnic conflict.

The world is losing control of its racial problems. The cause is a spiritual power that no legislation or human agency can stop. Only that which is bound in heaven can be bound upon the earth (see Matthew 18:18). If the church does not face the problem of overcoming racism within our own ranks and take spiritual authority over it, the world will soon fall into an abyss of chaos, destruction, and suffering of unprecedented proportions—all from racial conflict. The Lord stated in Luke:

> **"And there will be signs in sun and moon and stars, and upon the earth dismay among nations** [ethnos], **in perplexity at the roaring of the sea and the waves,**
>
> **men fainting from fear and the expectation of the things which are coming upon the world; for the powers of the heavens will be shaken"** (Luke 21:25-26).

As we see in Revelation 17:15, **"The waters which you saw. . . are peoples and multitudes and nations and tongues."** In the text from Luke we see that the **"roaring of the sea and the waves"** is caused by the turmoil among the ethnos, or ethnic conflicts. This situation will become so intense that men will faint from the fear of it. The problem will not go away with time, but will increase. The longer we wait to confront this stronghold, the more powerful it will become.

Ethnic pressure is now building in almost every major city in the world, but when it erupts it will not be confined to the cities. Even so, the Lord has demonstrated His power to calm the storm and the sea. King David declared of Him:

By awesome deeds Thou dost answer us in righteousness, O God of our salvation.

Who dost still the roaring of the seas, the roaring of their waves, and the tumult of the peoples (Psalm 65:5, 7).

The Lord will again stand up and calm the roaring sea with His word. The Lord came to destroy the works of the devil, and He has sent us with this same purpose. We are not here to stand and watch, but to stand against the darkness and push it back.

Racism is not just a demon, or even a principality—it is a "world ruler." It is one of the most powerful strongholds on earth, and it has sown more death and destruction than any other stronghold. Just consider the racial conflicts that have occurred recently! The most deadly wars in history, including World War II, were ignited by racism. This powerful spirit prepares the way for, and empowers, the spirit of death. This is why the Apostle Paul understood that when the ultimate racial barrier was overcome—the division between Jew and Gentile as they are grafted together in Christ—it would mean nothing less than **"life from the dead" (see Romans 11:15),** or the overcoming of death.

The Roots of Racism

Racism has two foundations. The first is pride, and its most base form is pride in the flesh. It is judging others by the externals, which is the ultimate form of pride. In its basic form, pride is simply feeling sufficient within ourselves and not recognizing our need for God or anyone else. This creates an obvious barrier between ourselves and others.

The second foundation of racism is fear. Insecurity is a result of the Fall and the separation between God and man. The insecure are afraid of those who are different. Racism is a powerful and deeply interwoven combination of both pride and fear. Trust is the bridge that makes relationships possible. You can have love, and even genuine forgiveness, but if you do not have trust, a lasting relationship is impossible. Fear and pride tear down the trust that makes relationships possible, thereby creating division.

The cross of Christ confronts and overcomes both the pride of man and his insecurity. One of the purposes for which the Holy Spirit was sent was to convict the world of sin, because it is the revelation of our sin that drives us to the cross to find grace and forgiveness. This destroys our pride by establishing our dependency on the Savior and restores our trust in Him.

The deeper the cross works in us, the more humble we will become, and the more secure we will be in His love. When we, who are so foreign to God's nature, are accepted back into fellowship with Him by His grace, a tolerance is worked in us for those who are different from our nature. Those who are becoming spiritually mature begin to judge from a spiritual perspective, not according to the flesh.

Therefore from now on we recognize no man according to the flesh; even though we have known Christ according to the flesh, yet now we know Him thus no longer.

Therefore if any man is in Christ, he is a new creature; the old things passed away; behold, new things have come (II Corinthians 5:16-17).

The church, above all, should not judge others according to the color of their skin or their cultural background. We must learn to see by the Spirit and judge only by the Spirit, just as it was said of Jesus:

And the Spirit of the Lord will rest on Him, the spirit of wisdom and understanding, the spirit of counsel and strength, the spirit of knowledge and the fear of the Lord.

And He will delight in the fear of the Lord, and He will not judge by what His eyes see, nor make a decision by what His ears hear (Isaiah 11:2-3).

If we are going to walk as He walked, we must learn to judge as He did: not making decisions by what our eyes see or by what our ears hear. This is the great lesson of the two men on the road to Emmaus. The resurrected Christ appeared to these disciples and preached to them about Himself for quite a while. This was Christ preaching Christ—it will never be more anointed than that! Yet they still could not recognize

Him because **"He appeared in a different form"** (see **Mark 16:12).**

One of the primary reasons why we often miss the Lord when He tries to draw near to us is that we tend to know Him after a form, rather than by the Spirit. If we are Charismatics, we tend to recognize Him only when He comes to us through a Charismatic. Or if we are Baptists, we tend to know Him only when He comes to us through a Baptist. However, He will usually approach us in a form that is different from what we are used to, just as He did with His disciples after the resurrection. This is because He is always seeking to have us know Him after the Spirit, not externals.

As the Lord declared: **"For I say to you, from now on you shall not see Me until you say, 'Blessed is He who comes in the name of the Lord!'"** (Matthew 23:39) We will not see Him until we learn to bless those that He sends to us, regardless of the form in which they come. Even Israel did not recognize the Lord when He came to them in a form that they were not expecting. This is not a new problem with God's people, but it is a serious one.

The Glory of Diversity

The church is called to have and to model the answers to the most fundamental human problems. Racism is one of the most basic and deadly problems in history and its power is greatly increasing at the present time. However, the church will stand out in stark contrast to the racist spirit of this age. That is why the Lord declared: **"My house shall be called a house of prayer for all the nations. . ."** (**Mark 11:17**). The church will not fulfill its destiny until it truly becomes a house of prayer for all ethnic peoples.

Paul said that, **"tongues are for a sign" (see I Corinthians 14:22)**. What sign? The sign that the church is to be the antithesis to the tower of Babel, where human languages were scattered and people were separated into different races and cultures. We see the first great demonstration of this sign on the day of Pentecost, at the very birth of the church:

> **Now there were Jews living in Jerusalem, devout men, from every nation under heaven.**
>
> **And when this sound occurred, the multitude came together, and were bewildered, because they were each one hearing them speak in his own language (Acts 2:5-6).**

The church is the place where men will be unified again, regardless of race, color, culture, or language. Is it not interesting that Jews from "every ethnos" heard and understood in one language? Jesus is the "Word of God" or God's communication to us (see John 1:1). When He is lifted up and men see His glory, all peoples will be drawn to Him and will understand with one heart again. The church that truly worships Him will be a demonstration of that reality.

As Paul told the Galatians, every member of the body of Christ—regardless of ethnic background or gender—has an equal standing before God.

> **For all of you who were baptized into Christ have clothed yourselves with Christ.**
>
> **There is neither Jew nor Greek, there is neither slave nor free man, there is neither male nor female; for you are all one in Christ Jesus (Galatians 3:27-28).**

There may be differences in our standing before God in such areas as governmental authority or specific ministries, but that has nothing to do with race, gender, or cultural background. Even the newest born-again Christian can go as boldly before the throne of God as the greatest preacher in the world. God does not show partiality. If we are walking by His Spirit, neither will we.

The Tyranny of the Familiar

The problem which I call "the tyranny of the familiar" is one of the strongest spiritual yokes that binds fallen human beings, and it continues to hinder the church. This yoke has baffled psychologists, who cannot understand why a high percentage of girls who grow up enduring the pain and torment of an alcoholic father will almost inevitably marry a heavy drinker. They choose the familiar path, painful and dangerous as it is, rather than the unpredictability of unfamiliar patterns that offer much more hope.

This same yoke to the familiar keeps many ethnic groups from breaking out of their sociological and economic barriers. In spite of the genuine frustrations and the talk of wanting a better life, most are afraid of change. Why is it that we so easily come into bondage to the familiar? Because we tend to put our security in our environment instead of in the Lord.

To institute true change, a strong trust must be built as a bridge out of our situation. Building this trust usually takes more time and effort than most people are willing to give. This is not a new problem. It is the same bondage the children of Israel succumbed to when they started desiring the flesh pots of Egypt over the supernatural provision of God. Jeremiah 48:11-12 addresses this issue in relation to the nation of Moab:

> **"Moab has been at ease since his youth; he has also been undisturbed on his lees, neither has he been emptied from vessel to vessel, nor has he gone into exile. Therefore he retains his flavor, and his aroma has not changed.**

> **"Therefore behold, the days are coming," declares the Lord, "when I shall send to him those who tip vessels, and they will tip him over, and they will empty his vessels and shatter his jars."**

When the Lord talks about being emptied from vessel to vessel, He is talking about change. This was how wine was purified in those times. It was poured into a vessel and allowed to sit for a time. As it sat, the impurities would settle to the bottom. Then it was poured into another vessel and was allowed to sit again so that the remaining impurities could settle. Therefore, the more the wine had been emptied from vessel to vessel, the purer it would become. Because Moab had not been subjected to the purifying changes, the "wine" of that nation was impure, and the Lord vowed to pour it out.

Although change is usually disconcerting, the Lord often brings radical changes to our lives so that we will be freed from the tyranny of the familiar. Every time the wine was poured into a new vessel, it was unsettled—there was a commotion and stirring which would bring out the remaining impurities. Whenever we are thrust into change, many things will begin to surface in our lives. Usually we will see very quickly just how much we have put our trust in the "vessel" that we are in instead of in the Lord. But we will settle down again, and we will become more pure because of this process. Change brings cleansing. That is one reason why the Lord kept Israel moving during most of its time in the wilderness.

The Wine of America

These same principles apply in a national situation. The difficulties encountered by black Americans provide a good example. Most of the problems of crime and violence in the inner cities can be traced to dysfunctional families. A high percentage of black families either have no father at home, or a father who is a poor role model. What is the root of this problem? In one word: slavery.

It is difficult for us to comprehend what it was like for a father to go to sleep each night knowing that he could be sold the next day, perhaps never to see his family again. His wife or children could also be sold, and he might never even know where they went. What would that do to the family? Fathers, mothers, and children could not really give their hearts to each other because of the terrible pain they would suffer if they were separated.

In 1712, a slave owner in the West Indies named Wilson Lynch wrote a letter to the British colonies in Virginia, devising a strategy for breaking up slave families so the slaves would be kept from rising in rebellion. He predicted that when the black family loyalties were destroyed, the only loyalty that the slaves would have would be to their owner. Lynch declared that when this strategy was implemented, it would destroy the fabric of black families for several hundred years. His diabolical prophecy came true. For generations, black women have had to be both the father and mother to their families, and they have found it difficult to accept the fathers in their rightful role. Fathers, likewise, have struggled to take their place.

If any other race or any other people had suffered the same historic problems as the black race, we would be having the same problems they are having now. I have actually heard many white leaders say that we would have no inner city problems "if blacks just had some ambition." But what do you think slavery did to the work ethic? Such deep cultural wounds cannot be healed without the intervention of the cross.

Blacks in America were allowed to be subject to slavery for the same reason that the Lord allowed Israel to become slaves in Egypt—they have a destiny in God. When they come into this destiny, the rest of America is going to be very thankful for this great and noble people in our midst. It is the destiny of the black race to carry freedom to a new level. This will be true freedom, with the dignity and honor that God created people to have.

The Power for Healing

It is by the Lord's stripes that we are healed (see I Peter 2:24 NKJV). In a sense, we, too, receive the authority for healing in the very place where we are wounded, once the wounds have been healed. Even after our wounds have been healed, there is still sensitivity in that area. Someone who has been subjected to abuse will be sensitive to others who have been abused. When someone who has been subjected to abuse is truly healed, not only will they themselves be free, but they will also have the authority to carry healing to others afflicted with those same wounds.

The black race is going to embrace the cross, receive healing for their wounds, and start loving white Americans with such a power that we will all be set free by that love. The Uncle Tom of *Uncle Tom's Cabin* truly was a prophetic figure. In spite of all the abuse that he suffered at the hands of his "owners," he was more free than they were, and he was willing to use his great freedom to lay down his own life if it would result in the salvation of others. The black believers in America, when they have been fully healed, will bring revival and true spiritual liberty to the whole nation.

The inner cities of America will ultimately become the inner sanctuary of God's tabernacle, the place where His glory and presence dwells. The greatest move of God that America has ever experienced will come out of the inner cities. The suburban churches may have the gold, but the inner city churches will make them jealous with His glory. If we are wise, we will take the gold that we have and use it to build the Lord a tabernacle not made with hands, but with people.

America is a nation that is made up of people from almost every other nation. This is the foundation of America's greatness, but it is also the foundation of our greatest problems. Even so, we have the potential to touch something of the glory of God that few other nations have. Our nation can potentially be the setting of another great Pentecost, for we, too, are a place where men have come to dwell "**. . . from every nation under heaven**" **(Acts 2:5).** This provides us with a great opportunity to demonstrate the solution to one of the world's most deadly problems, but will require us to be as the church was on the first Pentecost—"**all with one accord**" **(see Acts 2:1 NKJV),** or in unity.

America has come to a time in which we will have either the greatest victory or the greatest failure in the battle against racism. This powerful last day stronghold will either be defeated on our shores, or it will defeat us. America will either rise to even greater heights as a nation and a world leader, or it will fall like every previous great world power. If we do not embrace this glorious potential to defeat racism, we will be destroyed by the problems it brings.

When the Lord described the judgment, He said that He was going to separate the nations into "sheep" and "goats" (see Matthew 25:31-46). The sheep would go into His kingdom, and the goats would face eternal punishment. The distinguishing characteristics between them were that the sheep gave Him water when He was thirsty, gave Him food when He was hungry, and took Him in when He was "a foreigner" (see verse 35). When the sheep inquired about when they had done this, He answered: **"Truly I say to you, to the extent that you did it to one of these brothers of Mine, even the least of them, you did it to Me" (verse 40).**

One of the primary issues on which we will be judged will be our oneness with those who are different from us. Even the nations will be separated in this way. At the end of the age when many nations undergo a terrible destruction, there will also be some of the kingdoms of this world that have become kingdoms of our Lord (see Revelation 11:15). The nations that will be judged to be "sheep," so as to enter His kingdom, will be those who are open to the foreigners.

This is a fundamental issue on which we will all be judged, and it is a reason why the Lord has bestowed

His blessings upon America, and a number of other nations, to the degree that He has. Because racism deals with two of the most basic issues of the human heart, fear and pride, confronting this issue is one of the great opportunities that we have for entering His kingdom.

Humility is a basic characteristic that enables us to be open to those who are different from us. It also helps others to lower their defenses against us. Because God **"gives grace to the humble" (James 4:6)**, overcoming this problem opens us up like nothing else to the grace of God. When we add to this Christian love, being devoted to building up one another rather than tearing each other down, we are building upon the foundation of the kingdom.

Healing Cultural Wounds

Cultural sins are passed down from generation to generation until men arise to humble themselves and repent for the sins of their fathers. That is why we see so many biblical examples of this prayer of repentance for the sins of the forefathers, and it is usually prayed by the most righteous men, like Daniel, who had nothing to do with the sin. They simply understood this principle and were willing to stand in the gap for their people. This was the foundation of the cross, and is the true nature of Christ and those who would be Christlike.

Biblical repentance is more than just saying we're sorry, or even feeling sorry, it is turning from our evil ways. The white church in the South was one of the bastions that gave birth to the demented theologies and philosophies that justified and perpetuated slavery.

The Southern Baptist Convention was actually born in an attempt to justify and perpetuate the institution of slavery, although the denomination is quite different today. Many Southern Baptists are now on the very forefront of the war against racism, and the denomination has officially repented of its past racist actions. But the lingering effects of past racism by the Southern Baptist Convention, and most other denominations, are a primary reason why eleven o'clock on Sunday morning is still the most segregated hour of the week.

This is not meant to point the finger at any single group. The whole church has been a bastion of this most powerful stronghold of the enemy. That is one of the main reasons why we have so many denominations. However, the church will be free, and Southern Baptists will help to lead us out of this terrible darkness that is now sweeping the earth. The Southern Baptists are on the verge of a great revival, and it will be ignited by their unyielding assault on this terrible evil power of racism.

The white Southern Baptist church should have had the honor of doing what Martin Luther King, Jr. did—taking the leadership in this great battle against the world ruler of racism. Even so, the Southern Baptist church will take up the fight, and ultimately lead it. The Lord delights in redemption; it is His primary business. He is going to take what was meant for evil in the Southern Baptist Convention and use it for good, destroying the very evil that tried to use the church in this way.

The Light of the Church

Racism is one of the world's most serious problems, and we must show the world the solution. However, we will not have spiritual authority over the world's problems if we have the same strongholds in ourselves. We must recognize that the church today is still one of the most powerful bastions of racism. It is one of the most segregated institutions in the world. There are some notable exceptions to this, but generally it is true. Spiritual bigotry is just as prevalent as the natural form. Spiritual racism is at work when we judge other churches, movements, or people as inferior, or to be feared, because they are not a part of our group. This spiritual form of racism is a root cause of many of the present divisions in the body of Christ.

When Paul listed the qualifications for elders in the church, he specified that they had to be **"hospitable" (see Titus 1:8)**. In the original Greek, this actually means, "one who shows hospitality to aliens or foreigners." Basically he was saying that in order to be a leader of the church, a believer had to be open to those who were different. This perspective is fundamental to true spiritual leadership. One who is not open to those who are different is either too proud or too insecure to be in church leadership.

The Nature of Our Unity

While the whole world is degenerating into increasing chaos from its ethnic conflicts, the church is going to become increasingly unified. However, we must understand the nature of our unity. This does not mean that we all must become the same or submit to the same organizational structure. Just as a husband will never become one with his wife by trying to make her a man, we must see that our unity is based on the recognition and appreciation of our differences. The whole creation reflects the Lord's love for diversity. He makes every snowflake, tree, and person different. He desires to make every church different as well. However, these differences are not designed to conflict, but rather to complement one another. It is only because of our continued distance from the Lord, and the resulting insecurity, that we view these differences as threats.

This is not to imply that churches and movements will experience no conflicts over doctrinal or procedural differences. True unity does not come by compromising our convictions. Even so, most of the differences that bring conflict and division in the church are not serious enough for us to be divided over. In many cases, we resist the very ones we need the most—the ones God gives us to bring proper balance and perspective to our vision of the truth.

In my more than twenty years in the church, I have never witnessed a single division that was truly based on a commitment to truth. Men may have used doctrine or procedure as an excuse, but the real reason behind every split I have seen was territorial preservation—a most deadly and selfish evil in the church, and a major foundation of our spiritual racism. Racism empowers the spirit of death, and this spirit has probably killed more churches and movements than any other enemy. Until we are free of this enemy, we will not have spiritual authority over it in human affairs. The only answer for us and for the world is the cross. At the cross the dividing walls are taken down, and we are free to come into true unity.

One of the most significant barriers in the world today is between men and women. A man will never become the true man that he was created to be until he learns to properly relate to women, recognizing and appreciating their differences. Men will not have a true perspective on the Lord, the world, or anything else until we are open to the perspective that women have. The same is true for women—they need to have the benefit of the perspective of men. Therefore, to walk in truth, we need each other. A woman will never be all God has created her to be without learning to relate to men properly. In our society and in the church there are deep wounds remaining on the part of each, but there is healing for all of them at the cross. There is no true healing anywhere else.

No Charismatic, Pentecostal, Baptist, Methodist, or any other believer will fulfill his own destiny without a proper relationship to the rest of the church. Even though the high priest of Israel was from the tribe of Levi, he carried on his chest the stones of all the different tribes. This was to symbolize that those who would walk in the high calling must carry all of God's people on their hearts.

Only when we have been delivered from our own spiritual ethnic conflicts will we become **"a house of prayer for all the nations" (see Mark 11:17).** That is our fundamental calling. The times are about to press us into the desperation that is obviously required for us to become this. Let us not waste a day. Those who do not overcome the world will be overcome by it. When we begin to carry the cross, there is no spirit in this world that will not be subject to us. The cross has overcome the world and, when we embrace it, we, too, will overcome the world.

We will never have true unity until we can see each other with the Lord's eyes, hear each other with His ears, and love each other with His heart. Every human problem in the world is impossible for men to overcome until they embrace the cross. But how can we expect men to do this until we, the church, have done it? We can only bear true spiritual fruit to the degree that we are abiding in Jesus, the Vine (see John 15:15). The stronger our union is with Him, the more fruit we will bear.

The Lord Jesus did not judge by what He saw with His natural eyes or heard with His natural ears. His judgment was determined by what the Father revealed to Him. We cannot expect to walk in truth if we continue to get our discernment from the secular press, the evening news, or even what we see with our own eyes. There is always "a story behind the story" that only God knows, but He will reveal it to us if we turn to Him for our understanding.

Love and Revelation

In Deuteronomy 10:18-19, the Israelites were commanded to love the alien who was in their midst. Later, in Deuteronomy 31:12, they were commanded to teach the alien. There is a great revelation in this: We must love someone before we can teach them. True spiritual authority is founded upon love.

America is the most powerful nation on earth. It is also probably the most respected nation overall, and the most emulated. At the same time, in the eyes of many it is probably the most despised nation on earth. This hatred of America is not just jealousy. There is some basis for this hatred. It may be almost entirely unintentional, but we are continually offending and insulting other cultures. As a nation that has been truly made up of those from every other nation, we should be the last one to do this.

Almost sixty prime ministers and leaders of other nations have been educated in the United States, yet a high percentage of these were anti-American in their policy. The Japanese military leader who planned the attack on Pearl Harbor and the admiral who commanded the attack force were both educated at Harvard University! Could history have been different if we had treated these men with greater kindness while they were in our country?

Between two and three hundred thousand international students are presently being educated in the United States. These are usually the "cream of the crop" of their nation. Many of them are from nations where it is against the law to preach the gospel. We can reach the world without even leaving home just by showing hospitality to the foreigners who are presently on our campuses! They are usually isolated and lonely. Many of them have nowhere to go during holidays. Because of this, their time in the United States is often a negative experience. Many of these will one day be the leaders of their nations—some even prime ministers or foreign ministers. If the churches around these campuses would just reach out to these foreigners, the world could be greatly impacted.

The Ultimate Racist Barrier

The ultimate racist barrier is the barrier between Jew and Gentile. This is by God's design. The Jew is the natural seed of Abraham, and the church is the spiritual seed. Together they are meant to represent the heavens and the earth, which is why the promise to Abraham was that his seed would be as **"the stars of the heavens, and as the sand which is on the seashore" (see Genesis 22:17).** When the barrier between Jew and Gentile is overcome, it will signal the overcoming of the gulf between the spiritual and earthly realm so that God may establish His eternal habitation with man.

The Jews are the embodiment of the human spirit. They are a barometer of humanity, embattled within and without. As Paul said, **"From the standpoint of the gospel they are enemies for your sake..."** (Romans 11:28). They were hardened, or made hard to reach, for the sake of the gospel. The Jew represents the "acid test" of our message. Until we have a gospel that will make the Jew jealous, we do not yet really have the goods. That is why we are exhorted to preach the gospel to the Jew first. When we preach to the Jew, we will quickly find out the quality of our message.

The wounds that have been inflicted upon the Jews by the church are some of the deepest and most tragic in history. We have made our job much more difficult. To reach the Jews will require unprecedented humility on the part of the church, which will enable the Lord to extend unprecedented grace and trust us with an unprecedented anointing. That was precisely God's plan. We cannot fulfill our commission as the church without the Jews. They must be grafted back into the Vine.

The anointing required to bring the church to such a place of unprecedented humility and grace will cause every racist barrier in us to be overcome. That is why Paul could so confidently affirm that when this happened, it would release the ultimate grace on mankind: **"For if their rejection be the reconciliation of the world, what will their acceptance be but life from the dead?"** (Romans 11:15) The spirit of death, and the racism that empowers it, will be overcome when Jew and Gentile have been grafted into the Vine together.

The New Creation

The time during which the Lord dealt almost exclusively with the Jews was about 2,000 years. Likewise, the time of the Gentiles has now lasted nearly 2,000 years. What we are now coming into is not another time of the Jews, but rather a period in which both Jew and Gentile are grafted into one new creation through Christ.

True unity is in diversity, not in conformity. Converted Israel will not be like the church. The church is far from being what God created us to be, and so is Israel. When they are truly joined together, neither will be like they are now. We desperately need what the born-again Jew is going to bring into the church, but this does not imply a returning to the Law. The church will at last demonstrate on earth what the true new creation is—the union of the natural and spiritual seed of Abraham. This is the best wine, which the Lord has saved for last.

Many in the church have embraced a "replacement theology" that sees the church as a replacement of all the present purposes of God for Israel. Others have embraced a "replacement, replacement theology" that replaces the church with Israel. Both cloud the ultimate purpose for Israel and the church. In the Book of Romans, which is the most explicit book of New Covenant theology in the Scriptures, Paul clearly established God's purpose for each. He also warned against becoming **"arrogant toward the** [natural] **branches"** (11:18) and said, **"Do not be conceited,**

but fear; for if God did not spare the natural branches, neither will He spare you" (11:20-21). This is an issue of such importance that our failure here can cut us off from much of God's purpose.

This does not imply that we must accept everything that the earthly nation of Israel does. It is also clearly unbiblical to think the Jews can be grafted into the purpose of God in any way except through Christ. But speaking of the natural branches, Paul declared: **"I say then, God has not rejected His people, has He? May it never be!" (Romans 11:1)** For God to reject natural Israel would be to impugn the very integrity of His promises made to Abraham and then to others throughout the entire Old Testament. Most of these promises cannot reasonably be attributed to anyone but the natural Jew. As Paul asserted:

> **Then what advantage has the Jew? Or what is the benefit of circumcision?**
>
> **Great in every respect. First of all, that they were entrusted with the oracles of God.**
>
> **What then? If some did not believe, their unbelief will not nullify the faithfulness of God, will it?**
>
> **May it never be! Rather, let God be found true, though every man be found a liar, as it is written...** (Romans 3:1-4).
>
> **....from the standpoint of God's choice they are beloved for the sake of the fathers;**

For the gifts and the calling of God are irrevocable.

for just as you once were disobedient to God, but now have been shown mercy because of their disobedience,

so these also now have been disobedient, in order that because of the mercy shown to you they also may now be shown mercy.

For God has shut up all in disobedience that He might show mercy to all (Romans 11:28-32).

It will take extraordinary humility for the church to fully see God's purpose in natural Israel, and the same degree of humility will be needed for natural Israel to see God's purpose in the church. But this will happen, and when it does, it will release an unprecedented measure of God's grace to both.

Many believe that only converted Jews will be able to reach the Jews. This is contrary to His purpose, as well as to the biblical testimony of how God reaches people. The Lord sent Peter to the Jews and Paul to the Gentiles. According to our modern mentality, the Lord got this wrong. Certainly Paul, the Pharisee of Pharisees, would be better able to relate to the Jews. And Peter, the simple fisherman, would obviously be better able to reach the Gentiles. Although this is true in the natural, our gospel is not natural; it is spiritual, and the natural mind still cannot comprehend it.

The Lord sent Paul to the Gentiles because he was an offense to them. Therefore, the only way Paul could fulfill his commission was to be utterly dependent on the Holy Spirit—which is the only way the gospel is truly empowered. Likewise, the only way Peter could reach the Jews was to be utterly dependent on the Holy Spirit. This is true of all of us! Natural affinities do not help the gospel; they usually get in the way. **"That which is born of the flesh is flesh, and that which is born of the Spirit is spirit" (John 3:6).**

Just as the Lord humbled the Gentiles by sending them Jews, He is going to humble the Jews by sending them Gentiles. Of course, some Jews will have success in reaching their people, but generally this will not be the way in which they are reached. It is understandable that a Jewish convert would long to reach his own people. Paul did to the point that he was even willing to give up his own salvation. Even so, Paul was more effective in reaching the Gentiles because that was his commission. The Gentile church needs to take up the burden of reaching the Jews, and we desperately need the converted Jews to give input to the church.

The Distortion of Reality

The news media is one of the primary tools being used by the enemy to sow deception and division between peoples. Although this may not be their intent, it is the effect. The news itself is a gross distortion of reality. Only the most extreme events make the news, and most of them are acts of violence and destruction. Good news does not sell, and even when good news is reported it is not a true perception of reality. News of domestic violence is never balanced by news of the many happy families. The overwhelming majority of Americans will go about their business in a normal manner, but none of that which is "normal" America will make the evening news. The news itself presents a much distorted caricature of life in America, or anywhere else.

Even the Christian media, trying to do an honest job of reporting the interesting events in the church, often creates an unreal perception of Christianity for their readers. The average church in America is not like the churches that are newsworthy, but the day-to-day ministries of the average churches in their communities are probably doing far more to advance the gospel. These average churches are also a much more accurate reflection of the true state of Christianity today, for good or bad.

The very nature of the modern media distorts reality, even when this is totally unintentional. While the truly normal family would make a very boring television program, even the family-oriented sitcoms project an image of family life where almost every action or statement is either cute, funny, or dramatic. When the average family compares their lives to those of the television family, they often become disappointed with what they have and who they are. The overall effect of this is to blur reality and reduce our perceptions to "sound bites." We have been subtly trained only to respond to extremes.

Strongholds are basically lies that people believe. The more people who believe a falsehood, the more powerful that stronghold will be. The enemy is using the media to sow a demented perception of almost everything. The result will be that more and more of the extremes projected by the media will become "normal" behavior. Only the church, which has been given the Spirit of Truth, has the grace and power required to tear down these strongholds of misconceptions and false judgments. We must use the divinely powerful weapons with which we have been entrusted—weapons given to us for the purpose of tearing down strongholds and **"every lofty thing raised up against the knowledge of God" (see II Corinthians 10:5).**

The Deception of Extremes

One of Satan's greatest successes in bringing and maintaining division between people has been to keep us judging "people groups" by their most extreme elements. In this way, liberals look at conservatives and see the KKK. Conservatives look at liberals and see communists. It is a primary strategy of the enemy to have us perceive one another through the caricatures that he has sown in our minds. This drives us further apart and hinders the unity that the enemy fears so much.

Few Christians today are of the rabid nature demonstrated by many of the Crusaders, but the world nevertheless tends to view us all according to the most extreme elements of the faith. We must also recognize that very few members of other religions or ethnic groups are like the most extreme elements which we probably have viewed in the media.

Because the enemy's basic strategy is to sow division and misunderstanding by having us judge each other according to labels and stereotypes, we must overcome this by learning to judge other people after the Spirit and not after the flesh. We must increasingly get our discernment, and even our information, from the Holy Spirit rather than the news media.

Part II

THE STRONGHOLD OF WITCHCRAFT

Chapter Three
Overcoming Witchcraft

The practice of witchcraft has dramatically increased throughout the world in recent years. One of the expressed goals of this movement is to destroy biblical Christianity. Many Christians are presently suffering some form of attack from those who practice witchcraft. Discerning the nature of these attacks, and knowing how to overcome them, is becoming crucial for all believers.

We are exhorted not to be ignorant of the enemy's schemes (see II Corinthians 2:11). Peter warned us: **"Be of sober spirit, be on the alert. Your adversary, the devil, prowls about like a roaring lion, seeking someone to devour. But resist him, firm in your faith..." (I Peter 5:8-9).** Understanding Satan's schemes significantly increases our advantage in the battle. The entire church age has been one of spiritual warfare, which is increasing as we approach the end of the age. Those who refuse to acknowledge the reality of this warfare and fight against it are being quickly overcome.

Satan is now being cast out of the heavenlies and down to earth where he is coming with great wrath. Even so, we need not fear—He who is in us is much greater than he who is in the world (see I John 4:4). He who is least in the kingdom of God has more power than any antichrist. But just as the greatest military power today is vulnerable if it does not recognize the enemy's attack, we, too, are vulnerable if we do not recognize Satan's schemes. The only way he can defeat us is through our own ignorance or complacency. As we maintain our position in Christ, taking on the full armor of God and remaining vigilant, we will not only stand, but will prevail against the gates of hell.

What Is Witchcraft?

Witchcraft is counterfeit spiritual authority; it is using a spirit other than the Holy Spirit to dominate, manipulate, or control others.

In Galatians 5:20 the Apostle Paul named witchcraft, or **"sorcery,"** as one of the deeds of the flesh. Though witchcraft has its origin in the carnal nature of man, it usually degenerates quickly into demonic power. When we try to use emotional pressure to manipulate others, it is a basic form of witchcraft. When we use hype or soul power to enlist service, even for the work of God, it is witchcraft. When businessmen scheme to find pressure points while pursuing a deal, this also can be witchcraft. Many of the manipulative tactics promoted as sales techniques in marketing are basic forms of witchcraft. The primary defense against counterfeit spiritual authority is to walk in true spiritual authority. Establishing our lives on truth, and trusting in the Lord to accomplish what concerns us, are essential keys to becoming free from the influence and pressure of witchcraft.

It is written that Jesus is seated upon the throne of David. This is a metaphor, as Jesus does not sit upon the literal throne on which David sat. But David established a position of true spiritual authority that would ultimately be manifested in the kingdom of God. David did for spiritual authority what Abraham did for faith. How did David establish a seat of true authority? Basically, he refused to take authority or seek influence for himself, but completely trusted in God to establish him in the position that He had ordained for him. David did not lift his own hand to seek recognition or influence, and neither must we if we are going to walk in true spiritual authority rather than mere human political power.

Any authority or influence that we gain by our own manipulation or self-promotion will be a stumbling block to us, and will hinder our ability to receive true authority from God. If we are going to walk in true spiritual authority, like David, we will have to utterly trust in the Lord to establish us in it, in His time. As Peter exhorted, **"Humble yourselves, therefore, under the mighty hand of God, that He may exalt you at the proper time" (I Peter 5:6).**

Einstein once made an observation that may be more important than his theory of relativity, though it is utterly simple. He declared that, "Premature responsibility breeds superficiality." There is possibly nothing more devastating to our calling and potential for walking in true ministry than seeking influence or authority prematurely.

When the Lord promotes, He also supplies the grace and wisdom to carry the authority. There is no greater security available than knowing that God is the One who has established our ministry. Few things can breed insecurity faster than trying to maintain a position that we have gained by our own promotion or manipulation. This is the root of most of the territorial preservation and division that exists in the body of Christ.

Being established in true spiritual authority is a fortress that simply cannot be penetrated by the enemy. Paul explained that, **"the God of peace will soon crush Satan under your feet" (Romans 16:20).** When we know that we have been established by God, we have a peace that utterly crushes the enemy. In contrast, when we establish ourselves in a position of authority, we have little peace; the more our illegally gained influence increases, the more striving and manipulating it will take to hold it together. Anything that we do through manipulation, hype, or soul power, regardless of seemingly noble goals, is done in the counterfeit spiritual authority of witchcraft and is doomed to ultimate failure.

Therefore, the first principle in being delivered from the influence of witchcraft is to repent of all the ways that we have used it in our own lives and ministries. Satan cannot cast out Satan. Witchcraft, in even its most evil and diabolical forms such as black magic, will have an open door into our lives if we are using manipulation for controlling others or for gaining a position. Although we may try to justify using such devices in order to build the church, God is not fooled and neither is the enemy. What God is building is not raised up by might or by power, but by His Spirit. Whatever we build by any other means is an affront to the cross, and will ultimately oppose that which the Spirit is doing. The flesh wars against the Spirit, regardless of how good we try to make the flesh look.

Using the Gift of Discernment

Discernment of spirits is a primary gift of the Holy Spirit that enables us to distinguish the spiritual source of influences in the church. However, much of what is considered "discernment" today is really suspicion rooted more in fear and self-preservation than in the Holy Spirit. This is because so much of the authority that is exercised in the church today is counterfeit, which causes those who use it to be striving, fearful, and intimidated by anyone that they cannot control. True spiritual discernment is rooted in love that:

> **...is patient...kind...not jealous...does not brag and is not arrogant,**

does not act unbecomingly; it does not seek its own, is not provoked, does not take into account a wrong suffered,

does not rejoice in unrighteousness, but rejoices with the truth;

bears all things, believes all things, hopes all things, endures all things (I Corinthians 13:4-7).

Although we may be concerned that the readiness to bear, believe, hope, and endure all things will lead to naiveté rather than to discernment, the reverse is actually true. Unless we are seeing through the eyes of God's love, we are not seeing clearly, and we will not accurately interpret what we see. True discernment can only operate through God's love. This love is not to be confused with unsanctified mercy, which gives approval to things which God disapproves. Even though God's love is utterly pure and easily distinguishes between the pure and the impure, it does so for the right reasons. Insecurity, self-preservation, self-promotion, unhealed wounds, unforgiveness, bitterness, etc. will all confuse and neutralize true spiritual discernment.

Spiritual Maturity

Almost everyone in ministry must endure considerable rejection and misunderstanding. Learning to overcome rejection, by forgiving and praying for our persecutors just as the Lord did, is essential if we

are to walk in the Spirit and exercise true s͟
authority. If we are to accomplish the purposes oī
God, we must come to the level of maturity where, **"the love of Christ controls us" (see II Corinthians 5:14).** Love does not take into account the wrongs we have suffered and is not motivated by rejection, which drives us to retaliate or try to prove ourselves. Such reactions are the first steps in a fall from true authority. As the Lord Jesus stated:

> **"He who speaks from himself seeks his own glory** [literally "recognition"]; **but He who is seeking the glory** [recognition] **of the One who sent Him, He is true, and there is no unrighteousness in Him" (John 7:18).**

There are few things that will more quickly destroy our ability to walk in true spiritual authority than self-seeking, self-promotion, or self-preservation. Learning to deal with rejection is mandatory if we are to walk in a true ministry. Rejection provides an opportunity for us to grow in grace and die a little more to ambition, pride, and other motives which so quickly color our revelation. If we embrace rejection as the discipline of the Lord, we will grow in grace and love. If we rebel against this discipline, we may enter into witchcraft.

The Fear of Man Leads to Witchcraft

King Saul is a good example of how a man with a true commission from God can fall into this counterfeit spiritual authority. When he was commanded to wait for Samuel before offering the sacrifice, he succumbed to pressure and offered it prematurely, saying, **"I saw that the people were scattering from me. . . and that the Philistines were assembling..."** **(I Samuel 13:11).** Most that fall from true authority do so when they begin to fear the people or the circumstances more than they fear God. When we start to fear the people leaving more than we fear God leaving, we have departed from true faith.

Because witchcraft is basically rooted in the fear of man and **"the fear of man brings a snare" (see Proverbs 29:25),** those who begin to operate in witchcraft are trapped—fear has snared them. The bigger the project or ministry that we have built with hype, manipulation, or control spirits, the more we will fear anyone or anything that we cannot manipulate or control. Those who are caught in this deadly trap will most fear those who walk in the true anointing and authority. That is because those who walk in true spiritual authority are the least affected by the manipulation or spirit of control.

Saul became enraged at David and was consumed with destroying him, even though David was **"a single flea"** at the time (see I Samuel 24:14). As the manipulation and control spirits increase their dominion, so will the paranoia of those who are trapped in their grasp. Such people will become irrationally consumed by an attempt to drive out or destroy anyone who threatens their control. Those who receive their authority, recognition, or security from men will, like Saul, end up in the witch's house. That is why Samuel warned Saul that **"rebellion is as the sin of witchcraft"** (see I Samuel 15:23 NKJV). When one in spiritual authority rebels against the Holy Spirit, the void will be filled by the counterfeit spiritual authority of witchcraft. This may begin as a simple reliance upon hype and soul power, but without repentance it can end up in the most diabolical forms of presumption and rebellion, as we see in the case of King Saul. Persecuting those who were faithful to the Lord, Saul killed the true priests and spent one of his last nights in the house of a witch as the natural conclusion of the direction his life had taken.

Spiritual authority is a dangerous occupation. If we are wise, like David, we will not seek a position of authority, and we will not even take one which is offered until we are certain that the Lord is the one giving it. Satan tempts everyone called by God with the same temptation he offered to Jesus—if we will bow down to him and his ways, he will give us authority over kingdoms. God has called us to rule over kingdoms too, but His way leads to the cross. The authority He offers us can only be attained if we become servants of all. Satan's temptation is to offer the quick and easy path to the same place to which God has called us.

Presumption Kills

One of the most frequent phrases attributed to David's life was **"David inquired of the Lord"** (see I

Samuel 30:8). On the few occasions when David made a major decision without inquiring of the Lord, the consequences were devastating. The higher the position of authority, the more dangerous it is, and the more people are affected by even seemingly insignificant decisions. True spiritual authority is not an honor to be sought; it is a burden to be carried. Many who seek authority and influence do not know what they are asking for. Immaturity can be our doom if authority is given to us before our time.

Even though David lived a thousand years before the age of grace, he knew the Lord's grace and lived by it. Yet he still made mistakes which cost thousands of lives. It was probably because Solomon had observed this in his father that the one thing he desired was wisdom to rule over God's people. Anyone called to a position of leadership in the church must have the same devotion. Even if we are not in a position of spiritual authority, presumption can kill us. If we are in a position of authority, presumption will almost certainly lead to our fall, and can lead to the fall of many others as well.

The gift of a word of knowledge can be an awesome demonstration of power, but those who are called to walk in spiritual authority would do well to seek words of wisdom even more than words of knowledge. We need demonstrations of power and words of knowledge to accomplish the work of the Lord, but it is essential that we also have the wisdom to use them properly.

Humility Is a Safety Net

Those who attain prominence before humility will almost certainly fall. Therefore, if we have wisdom, we will seek humility before position. True authority operates on the grace of God, and the more authority we walk in, the more grace we will need. We only have true spiritual authority to the degree that the King lives within us. True spiritual authority is not position; it is grace. Counterfeit spiritual authority stands on its position instead of grace. The highest spiritual authority, Jesus, used His position to lay down His life. He commanded those who would come after Him to take up their crosses and do the same.

There is a simple distinguishing factor between the false prophets and the true. False prophets use their gifts, and the people, for themselves. True prophets use their gifts and give themselves for the people. Again, self-seeking, self-promotion, and self-preservation are the most destructive forces to true ministry. Like King Saul, even if we have been anointed by God, we can fall to witchcraft if these forces gain control over us.

Protection from Charismatic Witchcraft

Not only must those in leadership be wary of using witchcraft, they must also be aware that they will be the primary targets of those who do. Witchcraft is an enemy we must guard against from within and without. It is just as subtle when it attacks from without as when it takes ground from within. This form of sorcery is seldom what we call black magic, but is usually a form of "white witchcraft." Those who practice it are often well-meaning people who do not have the confidence to be straightforward, and have, therefore, fallen to subtle forms of manipulation to gain influence.

One prominent form of white witchcraft, which is common in the church, can be described as "charismatic witchcraft." This is a pseudo spirituality used to gain influence or control by wearing a super spiritual mask. This is a source of false prophecies, dreams, and visions which can ultimately destroy or neutralize a church, or bring the leadership to the point where they overreact so as to despise prophecy altogether. Those using this form of witchcraft almost always think that they have the mind of the Lord, and therefore conclude that those in leadership are the ones in rebellion.

Jezebel

Jezebel, who is one of the archetypes of witchcraft in Scripture, used her power to control her husband, who had authority over Israel. She was also able to bring such depression upon Elijah that he sought death over life, even after his greatest spiritual victory. There is great power in this evil; those who are ignorant of it, or who presumptuously disregard its potential to affect them, are very often brought down by it, usually without ever knowing what hit them.

Ahab may have easily been overpowered, but Elijah was certainly no wimp. He had just single-handedly confronted and destroyed more than eight hundred false prophets. This was one of the greatest demonstrations of God's power over evil in all of history. Yet after this, one woman operating in the power of witchcraft was able to send the great prophet fleeing in discouragement.

How could this happen? Compared to the power of God, all the power of the evil one would not even register on the scale! The newest babe in Christ has more power dwelling in him than all of the antichrists put together. How is it that we are still overcome by evil? It is because Satan does not confront God's people with power; he seduces them with deception.

Compared to the eight hundred false prophets, who was this one woman to challenge Elijah? Certainly he could have destroyed her power even more easily than he had destroyed theirs. It was not rational for Elijah to have become so discouraged because of Jezebel's threat, but that is precisely the point: This attack did not come through reasoning; it was a spiritual attack. Reasoning usually has little to do with the power of witchcraft.

Jezebel slammed Elijah immediately after his greatest victory, and he was overpowered. We will often be most vulnerable to this attack after a great victory, because it is then that we tend to drop our guard and be the most open to pride. So, our first defense against the attacks of the enemy through witchcraft, or any other tactic, is to maintain the humility of knowing that we are standing only by God's grace. Pride leaves a breach in our armor that the enemy can easily penetrate.

Chapter Four
The Stinger

The attacks of witchcraft come in a series of stings. The successive stings are meant to hit the very places where we have been weakened by the previous stings. In this way, they build upon each other until the cumulative effect overwhelms the target. The stings of witchcraft usually come in the following order:

1. Discouragement

2. Confusion

3. Depression

4. Loss of vision

5. Disorientation

6. Withdrawal

7. Despair

8. Defeat

This process can happen quickly, as it did with Elijah, but it usually works more slowly, which makes it even more difficult to discern. However, if we know the enemy's schemes we will not continue to be subject to them. When these symptoms begin to make inroads into our lives, we must resist the enemy until he flees. If we do not resist him, we will be the ones fleeing, just like Elijah.

The source of the witchcraft used against us may not be the obvious satanic cults or New Age operatives. It can come from well-meaning, though deceived, Christians who are, in effect, praying against us instead of for us. These misguided prayers have power, because whatever is released on earth is released in heaven, and whatever is bound on earth is bound in heaven. If intercession is motivated by a spirit of control or manipulation, it is witchcraft, and its power is just as real as that of black magic.

Other sources of charismatic witchcraft can be such things as gossip, political maneuvering, and jealousy, and they can have an effect on us whether we allow ourselves to be manipulated by them or not. For example, consider the result if we refuse to be manipulated by someone who has a control spirit, but allow ourselves to become resentful or bitter toward that person. In such a case, the enemy has still caused us to fall, and the same discouragement, disorientation, and depression will come upon us just as surely as if we had submitted to the control spirit.

We are defeated by the enemy when he can get us to respond in any spirit other than the Holy Spirit, whose fruit is love, joy, peace, etc. (see Galatians 5:22-23). The enemy's strategy is to cause us to depart from the fruit of the Holy Spirit, and try to combat him on his own terms. Satan cannot cast out Satan; resentment will never cast out Jezebel—it will only increase her power. That is why the basic strategy we must use to begin freeing ourselves from the power of witchcraft is to bless those who curse us. This does not mean that we bless their works, but that we pray for them and not against them. If the enemy can get us to retaliate, he will then have us using the same spirit, and we will have multiplied the very evil we were trying to cast out. We are not warring against flesh and blood, and the weapons of our warfare are not carnal, but spiritual. When we begin to pray blessing upon the people who are attacking us, then the evil power of control and manipulation is broken over both them and us. We must not return evil for evil, but we must overcome evil with good.

Discerning the Stings of Witchcraft

Sting 1—DISCOURAGEMENT

Everyone gets discouraged at times, and it can be for many different reasons, so this is not always the result of witchcraft being used against us. But if we become subject to increasing discouragement for no apparent reason, witchcraft should be considered as a possible source. When your difficulties seem insurmountable and you want to give up, even though matters are really not any worse than usual, you are probably coming under spiritual attack. The enemy's attempt to afflict you with discouragement is meant to weaken you for the next level of attack, which is:

Sting 2—CONFUSION

Again, we must look for a general and increasing "spirit of confusion" for which there is no apparent reason. Here we begin to lose our clarity as to what we have been called to do, which of course will weaken our resolve. This confusion is meant to compound our discouragement, making us even weaker and more vulnerable to further attack, which will usually come in the form of:

Sting 3—DEPRESSION

This is a deeper problem than simple discouragement. It is an unshakable dread that comes as a result of the combined effect of discouragement and confusion, along with a general negligence of spiritual disciplines that has usually slipped in by this time. This will become an increasingly prevalent problem in the last days, and we must gain the victory over it. If we do not, it will quickly lead to the next sting:

Sting 4—LOSS OF VISION

This is the goal of the previous stings, and it works to increase their effect. Here we begin to doubt that God has called us to the task in the first place. The only way that we can sail through the storm of confusion is to hold our course, but we cannot hold our course if we do not know where we are going. We will not try to hold our course if we begin to think it was wrong for us to ever pursue our vision in the first place. Such a loss of vision will lead to our drifting in circles at the time when we most need to **"make straight paths for** [our] **feet" (see Hebrews 12:13).** This sets us up for the next level of assault:

Sting 5—DISORIENTATION

The combined result of depression, confusion, and loss of vision is usually disorientation. By this time, not only have we forgotten the course we are supposed to be holding, but we have even lost our ability to read the compass. The Scriptures will no longer speak to us, and it is a struggle to trust the Lord's voice or receive much encouragement from even the most anointed teaching or preaching. This is the point of spiritual incapacitation, which results in:

Sting 6—WITHDRAWAL

When disorientation sets in, it is tempting to withdraw or retreat from our purpose in the ministry, our fellowship with the rest of the church, and often from our families and others we are close to. This withdrawal will result in:

Sting 7—DESPAIR

Withdrawal from the battle leads quickly to hopelessness and despair. Without hope we can easily be taken out by the enemy, either through temptation, sickness, or death. Science has proven that when hope is removed, even the healthiest person will quickly deteriorate and die. But with hope, men and women have lived long past the point when a normal body would have quit. Despair will always lead to:

Sting 8—DEFEAT

Spiritual Amalekites

The enemy's purpose is to weaken us so that we begin to fall further and further behind; then we can be picked off more easily. In Scripture, the Amalekites were typical of Satan and his hordes. It was the practice of the Amalekites to attack the weak and the defenseless. As the camp of Israel crossed the wilderness, the Amalekites picked off the loners or stragglers who fell behind the rest of the camp.

This is what the enemy seeks to do through witchcraft. He seeks to weaken believers so that they will begin to fall behind the rest of the camp and become easy prey. This is why Israel was told that there would be perpetual war with the Amalekites. When Israel's kings were commanded to fight them, they were also commanded to utterly destroy them and not take any spoil. We have a perpetual war against Satan, and we cannot take any prisoners. Neither can we use that which is his in the service of God.

King Saul disobeyed this command. He kept alive Agag, king of the Amalekites, and kept some of the spoil **"to sacrifice to the Lord"** (see **I Samuel 15:15**). This represented a failure of the most foolish kind for one called to lead God's people. In those days, keeping a rival king alive after a battle was only done for one of two reasons: to make him an ally or a slave. Saul foolishly thought that he could make the one who personified Satan himself into an ally or a slave.

It was no accident that it was an Amalekite who killed Saul and carried the news of Saul's death to David. This Amalekite thought that the news would be pleasing to David, but David was discerning and had him killed (see II Samuel 1:1-16). If we do not obey the Lord and utterly destroy the enemy we battle, he will end up finishing us off. There can be no alliance with the enemy; he and his hordes must be utterly destroyed. Neither let us be foolish enough to think that we can use the enemy as our slave; in his guile he will quickly turn the tables.

Witchcraft is being used against the church. Many who have failed to recognize it have been defeated, losing their vision, their ministry, their families, and even their lives. This is not sensationalism; it is fact. Paul said that we do not wrestle against flesh and blood, but against principalities and powers (see Ephesians 6:12). Wrestling is the closest form of combat. The enemy is going to fight; he is going to wrestle with us. If we decide that we just are not going to fight, we will get pinned! As Christians we have no option as to whether or not we are going to do spiritual warfare; if we want to survive, we must fight. But how do we combat this witchcraft? We must first look at the basic principle of spiritual warfare required for every victory.

The Road to Victory

In Revelation 12:11 we see that the saints overcome Satan:

1. By the blood of the Lamb,

2. By the word of their testimony, and

3. By loving not their lives even unto death.

We overcome by the blood of the Lamb as we take our stand on what He has already accomplished for us by the cross. The victory has already been won, and there is no way we can lose if we abide in Him.

The word of our testimony is the Scriptures. Every time the enemy challenged Jesus, He simply responded with Scripture, countering the enemy's temptation with God's truth. The Word of God is **"the sword of the Spirit" (see Ephesians 6:17).** With the sword we can deflect the blows from his deceptive words, as well as attack him. Of all the pieces of armor we are commanded to use (see Ephesians 6:10-18), the sword is the only offensive weapon.

That they **"loved not their lives unto the death," (Revelation 12:11 KJV)** is the utter commitment to follow Him regardless of the price. We are called to take up our crosses daily; to do all things for the sake of the gospel; to no longer live for ourselves but for Him. To the degree that we remain in self-centeredness, we will be vulnerable to the enemy's attack. When we have reckoned ourselves dead to this world, as crucified with Christ, then the enemy no longer has any access to us because he has no more access to Him. If we are dead to this world, then what can be done to a dead person? It is impossible for the dead to be offended, to be tempted, to fear, to be depressed, or to be continually looking for the easy way out, since they have already paid the ultimate price.

All of these—the blood of the Lamb, the word of our testimony, and a commitment to lay down our lives—are required for spiritual victory. Anything less will fail to bring a complete victory. We may make occasional, halting advances, but we will sooner or later be pushed back. However, it is clear that at the end of the age an army of believers will be raised up who will not settle for occasional advances—they have committed themselves to the fight, and will not stop until there is total victory. **"The earth is the Lord's, and all it contains. . ." (Psalm 24:1).** Until the earth has been completely recovered from the domain of Satan, our fight is not over.

No one will fight to win if they do not believe victory is possible. Many teachings have been promulgated that declare the church's defeat before Christ's return. Yet the whole prophetic testimony of Scripture is that the Lord, the church, and the truth are going to prevail. Satan is indeed being cast down to the earth, bringing with him a time of trouble like the world has never known before—but we will still win!

Isaiah 14:16-17 says that when we see Satan we are going to marvel at the pitiful nature of the one who caused so much trouble! He who lives within the very least of the saints is much greater than the combined power of all the antichrists. These times are not to be feared—this will be our finest hour! As Isaiah 60:1-2 declares, when darkness is covering the earth, the glory of the Lord will be appearing on His people. The darkness will just make His glory upon us appear that much brighter. We must start fighting in order to win, giving no more ground to the enemy, and taking back what he has usurped.

To effectively combat witchcraft, we must determine that we are going to resist Satan until he flees from us. Our goal is more than just driving the enemy out of our own lives; we then must pursue him until he is driven out of others in whom he has established a stronghold. The following are some of the ways we can combat and overcome the eight specific areas of Satan's attack through witchcraft.

Resisting the Stings of Witchcraft

1) Overcoming Discouragement

Discouragement never comes from God; He is the Author of faith and the Source of hope which never disappoints. Although God does discipline us when we need it, He never does so by afflicting us with discouragement. When James describes the wisdom that comes from above, he does not list discouragement as one of the characteristics: **"But the wisdom from above is first pure, then peaceable, gentle, reasonable, full of mercy and good fruits, unwavering, without hypocrisy" (James 3:17).** Discouragement is, in fact, the very opposite of the love, joy, peace, and other attributes of the Holy Spirit's fruit (see Galatians 5:22-23).

We must learn to quickly and instinctively reject discouragement, giving it no place in our thoughts. We must tenaciously resist it, taking every thought captive to obey Christ (see II Corinthians 10:5). Discouragement must never be allowed to dictate our course. Faith is the fruit of the Spirit and the shield of our armor that counters discouragement. If we begin to get discouraged, it is because we have dropped our shield. We need to pick it back up!

2) Overcoming Confusion

"God is not the author of confusion" (see I Corinthians 14:33), so we can know for certain that when confusion strikes, it is not coming from Him. In the military, confusion is one of the primary elements of battle that a soldier is trained to handle. Since nothing will ever go exactly as planned, there will rarely be a battle where there is not confusion— and the same is true in spiritual warfare.

The disciplined soldier who understands this aspect of warfare learns to use the confusion to his own advantage. He does not let it increase his discouragement, but begins to anticipate it, looking for an opportunity to gain an advantage over the enemy. We must learn to expect confusion as part of the battle and not to be surprised or affected by it. Our resolve to stand and fight will quickly dispel this aspect of the attack.

3) Overcoming Depression

God told Cain the most effective remedy for depression:

> **Then the Lord said to Cain, "Why are you angry? And why has your countenance fallen?**
>
> **"If you do well, will not your countenance be lifted up? And if you do not do well, sin is crouching at the door; and its desire is for you, but you must master it" (Genesis 4:6-7).**

Depression is usually the result of allowing discouragement and confusion to cause us to drift from our basic spiritual disciplines, such as reading the Word, praying, fellowshiping, etc. The downward spiral almost always starts to reverse when we cast off any negative attitudes and again commit ourselves to these disciplines.

4) Overcoming a Loss of Vision

This attack can also be turned to our advantage and used as an opportunity. When we begin to lose our vision, we must commit ourselves to strengthening our vision more than ever. We need to sink our roots deeper, and establish our purpose even more firmly upon the Word of God. When God begins to lead us into a purpose, we should record how He speaks to us. By searching the Scriptures and reviewing all the ways He has led us in the past, we will even more firmly establish His leading.

Above all, we must hold our course! We should not change our direction until we can clearly see the new course. In World War I, one of the most effective tactics of the enemy was to lay a smoke screen in front of Allied battleship convoys. As the convoy entered the smoke, visibility was lost. The ships would start turning at any perceived sound or whim, with the resulting collisions sinking more ships than the enemy torpedoes did.

The Allies finally developed a simple strategy to thwart this tactic against their "vision": When in the smoke, every ship was to hold its previous course without deviation. By so doing, they discovered that they would soon all sail out the other side, into clear air. The same strategy will enable us to more quickly escape whatever is clouding our vision. When we lose our vision, we need to hold our course and keep moving forward. We will soon break out into the clear.

5) Overcoming Disorientation

As an instrument flight instructor, the first thing I had to teach a student pilot was that when flying on instruments with restricted visibility, he must not trust his feelings. If a pilot tries to fly by his feelings when in instrument conditions, he will quickly lose control of the plane. Even when flying perfectly straight and level through the clouds, it can begin to feel like the plane is turning. If the pilot reacts to this feeling, he will begin to turn in order to counteract this supposed drift—causing the plane to veer off course or possibly even turn upside down.

In a test conducted by the FAA, a group of pilots without previous instrument training were flown into instrument conditions. Every one of them lost control of their planes because they tried to rely on their feelings for guidance. The same is true of immature Christians who enter spiritual conditions of reduced visibility, or "spiritual clouds." They usually try to rely on their feelings for guidance, and therefore lose control.

The "instruments" we have been given to walk by are found in the Bible. We do not walk by feelings but by faith in the sure testimony of the Word of God. The Word of God will keep us oriented and on course if we put our trust in it, even when our feelings may be telling us to do otherwise.

6) Overcoming Withdrawal

In the Persian Gulf War, the majority of casualties were either reserves or civilians. The safest place to be in the war was on the front line. This has been true in most modern wars, and it is true in spiritual warfare as well.

When we are being pressed in a battle, we cannot call a time-out. On the frontline we cannot ask the enemy to stop the battle because we have a headache or want to take a break. When we are on the front line, we know the dangers and do not let our guard down. Every Christian is on the front line every day, whether he likes it or not. Satan will not stop when we call a time-out. It is when we start to consider ourselves "civilians," or not soldiers, that we will be the most vulnerable to his attack. Neither is a Christian ever in the reserves. Yes, there are times of reprieve from conflict, for seldom do battles continually rage along the entire front. But when we know that we are on the front, even our breaks are taken with vigilance, realizing that a fresh attack can come at any time. Christians must never remove their spiritual armor, and must never lose their vigilance.

In times of warfare, there are occasions when a strategic retreat is necessary. At times we have overcommitted ourselves spiritually and must draw back—but that is not the same as withdrawing from the battle. Even when we have overcommitted ourselves, retreat should be a last resort, for an army in retreat is in its most vulnerable condition. If at all possible, we should at least try to hold our ground until our position can be strengthened.

Even when we discover that in a certain matter we have acted presumptuously, without being commissioned by God, we must not quit; we should repent. There is a difference between quitting and stopping because of repentance. The first is a defeat; the latter is an adjustment that will always result in further victories. Repentance comes because of the truth that sets us free; defeat will result in a spiritual bondage to the power of the enemy.

7) Overcoming Despair

In Genesis 2:18, the Lord said that it was not good for man to be alone. We are social creatures, and when we withdraw from fellowship we usually sink into the deepest pit of hopelessness—despair. At this point in the downward spiral, we must return to fellowship and get help in reversing the slide, or else we will be defeated. As simple as this may seem, it is the remedy. Even though fellow believers can be the source of the enemy's attack on us, we must never run away from the church. We must run to it, and work out our problems until they are resolved.

8) Overcoming Defeat

Even if Satan's stings of witchcraft have brought such devastation to our lives that we are temporarily defeated, we must see that God can still bring us to ultimate victory. Paul commented to the Corinthians that he had been **"struck down, but not destroyed" (see II Corinthians 4:9)**. At one point, Paul faced such severe attacks that he **"despaired even of life,"** but through it all he learned that the secret of regaining victory was not in trusting in himself but in **"God who raises the dead" (see II Corinthians 1:8-9)**.

Paul wrote, **"but thanks be to God, who gives us the victory through our Lord Jesus Christ" (I Corinthians 15:57)** and **"but in all these things we overwhelmingly conquer through Him who loved us" (Romans 8:37)**. Defeat is not an option in Christ. We will gain the victory in that which He has called us to do. The only way we can be defeated is to quit.

Chapter Five

Combating New Age Witchcraft

The New Age movement is basically a combination of witchcraft and Hinduism, disguised to make it acceptable to white-collar professionals. There is an important reason why this form of spiritualism is targeting this group. For almost 5,800 years of the earth's 6,000 years of recorded history, nearly 95 percent of all workers were agricultural. In just a little over a century, that statistic has been reversed so that now less than 5 percent of the workers in the Western nations are agricultural. This change was the result of technological advances. The 5 percent who work in agriculture now produce more than the 95 percent could in the last century.

In the mid 1950s, white-collar workers exceeded the number of blue-collar workers in the West. Since that time, this majority has grown until it is now estimated that blue-collar workers will go the way of agricultural workers in the near future, composing only a very small fraction of the population. When it was predicted that **"knowledge will increase"** in the end times (see Daniel 12:4), few could have comprehended the degree to which this would happen. Information is now the most valuable commodity in the world, and the job of accumulating, interpreting, packaging, and transferring knowledge is the world's largest industry.

Those involved in the "knowledge industry" are not only the most numerous; they are also the wealthiest and most powerful. They are a group that the church has become increasingly unsuccessful in reaching, which has made them an appealing target for the New Age movement and other cults. Man was created to have fellowship with God, who is Spirit, and because of this there is a spiritual void in man that hungers for the supernatural.

The day of supernatural neutrality is over. Those who do not know the true supernatural power of God will become increasingly subject to the evil and counterfeit supernatural powers of the enemy. Those whose fears or doctrines have led them to avoid the supernatural power of God will find themselves, and especially their children, easy prey to evil supernatural power.

Kingdoms in Conflict

Paul explained, **"For the kingdom of God does not consist in words, but in power"** (**I Corinthians 4:20**). Satan knows this, and is therefore quite content to fight the battle on the level of words and doctrines. Regardless of how accurately we can argue doctrinal positions, Satan will have little problem conquering us if we do not know the power of God, which is a fundamental aspect of God's kingdom. Those who really believe the Bible will walk in power. Righteousness is the result of believing in our hearts, not just in our minds, and those who do not know the power of God only believe Him in their minds.

Considering the foolish antics often characterizing those of us who have known the power of God in the Pentecostal, Charismatic, Full Gospel, and Third Wave movements, it is easy to understand why many would shy away from the gifts of the Spirit. But this, too, is one of the tests that separates the true believers from those who just know creeds or doctrines. God has called the foolish things of the world to confound the wise. Only the humble will come to what He is doing, and He will give His grace only to them.

Churches which have rejected the supernatural power of God have become increasingly irrelevant and unable to reach the world, for the battle for men's souls is intensely supernatural in nature. The more secularized society becomes, the more it actually magnifies people's hunger for the supernatural. That is why atheists tend to be drawn to the most base forms of witchcraft and the black arts, which they are deceived into thinking are powers resident within man, when actually the powers are demonic in nature. The denominations and movements within the church which have rejected the power of God are almost all shrinking, as they have become irrelevant and boring, with little or no power to attract converts.

Many of the churches and denominations that have rejected the power of God have already succumbed to influences from the New Age movement. Others are succumbing to the spirit of the age in other forms, not only tolerating the perverted and unbelievers as members, but actually ordaining them as pastors and leaders. Contrary to this, the denominations and movements that preach and walk in the supernatural power of God are not only growing, but are by far the fastest growing religious movements in the world.

Paul the apostle declared:

> **And my message and my preaching were not in persuasive words of wisdom, but in demonstration of the Spirit and of power,**
>
> **that your faith should not rest on the wisdom of men, but on the power of God (I Corinthians 2:4-5).**

The conflict between the kingdom of God and the kingdom of evil is not just a conflict between truth and error (though it is that, too); it is also a confrontation of supernatural powers, with both sides seeking to fill the spiritual void in man created by the Fall.

The entire history of God's dealings with mankind has involved demonstrations of supernatural power. It is incongruous to say we are a biblical people and yet not walk in the supernatural power of God. True Christianity is not just a matter of words; it is a demonstration of God's love and power to save, heal, and deliver. Jesus stated that as the Father sent Him into the world, He has sent us into the world (see John 17:18). As our example, Jesus did not just talk about God's power to heal and save, He demonstrated it. If we are going to preach the gospel, we must preach it as He did, demonstrating both God's love and His power. When Jesus sent out His disciples to preach the kingdom, they were to heal the sick and cast out demons (see Luke 9:12). The Lord never changes, nor does He change the way He sends His true messengers.

Many of the biblical prophecies concerning the end of the age address the supernatural nature of the conflicts that will occur. A church that does not walk in God's power will become increasingly inadequate to deal with the times and confront the powers that come against it. To overcome the increasing power of the enemy we must **"desire earnestly spiritual gifts, but especially that you may prophesy" (see I Corinthians 14:1). "God is spirit, and those who worship Him must worship in spirit and truth" (John 4:24).** Again, the first defense against the deceptive supernatural power of the enemy is to know the true power of God.

Most believers have some desire for spiritual gifts, but we must **"earnestly"** desire them if we are going to receive them. Even though most of the church is now "open" for God to use them in a demonstration of His power, He has decreed that we must ask, seek, and knock in order to receive (see Matthew 7:7). Those who are just "open" for the Lord to use them are rarely used. Being "open" is usually a cop-out for those who are either too fearful or too prideful to risk failure. It takes faith and persistent seeking if we are to receive.

Pious Delusions

It is often repeated that we are to seek the Giver and not the gifts. That sounds pious, but it is not biblical. Certainly we are to seek the Giver more than the gifts, but we are commanded to seek the gifts, too—the two are not mutually exclusive. Seeking to walk in the gifts of the Spirit is actually one form of seeking God, and even more important, it is being obedient. Many such glib statements of apparent wisdom are merely human wisdom, and are often in conflict with the Scriptures.

Our God is supernatural, and we cannot truly desire fellowship with Him without desiring fellowship with the supernatural. While many Christians have been hardened by doctrines that justify their powerlessness, claiming that God no longer moves supernaturally, they still long in their hearts for the supernatural. We were all created for fellowship in the Spirit, which is by definition supernatural.

Recently, some of the world's most brilliant theologians and apologists for why God no longer works supernaturally have been won over and are now walking in God's power themselves, often after witnessing just one genuine miracle. Genuine is the key word here. Those who sincerely love God and seek to walk in His power are turned off by the fakery and hype often associated with the ministries of those who really do not yet have God's power.

The True Gospel

True Christianity is the true Word of God verified by the true power of God. Jesus went about to **"do and teach" (see Acts 1:1).** He usually performed miracles before He taught. He knew that people who had an undeniable encounter with God were going to be far more open to what He would say to them. The power Jesus and His apostles demonstrated was used to confirm and illuminate their teaching. The same is still true; the demonstration of God's power transforms intellectual concepts into a true faith in the teachings of the Lord. It takes both the Word and the power of God to change the inner man. Without both, we may change our outward behavior, but our hearts remain untouched. It is the spiritual void in the heart that must be filled by a true fellowship with God if we are going to be free from the spiritual influence and power of the enemy.

Because witchcraft is counterfeit spiritual authority, we will only be completely free from the power of witchcraft when we are completely submitted to the authority of God. If the spiritual void that is in us is not filled with the real power and authority of God, we will become subject to witchcraft in some form as we draw closer to the end of the age. The Battle of Armageddon is fought in the **"valley of decision"** (**see Joel 3:14**); everyone on earth will be brought to the place of making a decision. It is a power confrontation, and the choice is being made concerning issues of power and authority. We will choose either the power and authority of God or the power and authority of the evil one—but we will all choose.

Discerning Counterfeits

All of the spiritual gifts available to the church are presently being counterfeited by the enemy. Ironically, those whose lack of faith causes them to avoid spiritual gifts in order to keep from being deceived are certain to be deceived. We must walk by faith, not fear, if we are going to stay on the path that leads to life. Fear will inevitably lead us to deception if we allow it to be our motivation.

If we are going to fulfill the purpose of God, it will take a faith like Abraham's, willing to risk leaving everything behind in order to seek that which He is building. If we are going to walk in the power of God, we must have more faith in God to lead us into all truth than we do in the enemy's ability to deceive us. Faith is the door to fellowship with God, because it takes faith to reach beyond the natural realm to the supernatural, so that we can see **"Him who is unseen"** (**see Hebrews 11:27**).

As we walk in faith, that which we begin to see with the eyes of our hearts will become more real to us

112

than what we are seeing with our natural eyes. Then we will begin living more for the eternal than for the temporal. Those who walk in true faith are naturally going to appear foolish to those who live according to the wisdom of this world, or those who are of a "natural mind."

We take a major step in being delivered from the power of witchcraft when we start to see the Lord so clearly that we respect and serve Him more than anything else. Then we are no longer subject to the influence, manipulation, and control of those who are still earthly-minded, or who move in the power of witchcraft.

Those who give themselves to becoming authorities on the nature of evil almost always become darkened and evil in nature themselves. Many "cult watchers" have released an even more foul spirit in the church than the cults they were watching. The paranoia they have promulgated has done more to bring division and damage to the church than any cult has been able to do. These have often become the faultfinders that Jude talked about, printing and distributing slander and gossip as if it were researched fact. As Jude warned, these are being reserved for the **"black darkness" (see Jude 10-16),** in which many of them have already begun to live.

We do not need to study the darkness as much as we need to study the light. Light will always overpower darkness. If we walk in the light, we will cast out the darkness. If we walk in the true supernatural power of

God, we will overpower the evil supernatural power as surely as Moses confounded the sorcerers of Egypt. But Moses would not have been successful had he gone to Egypt with no power, and neither will we succeed in setting people free today if we are powerless. The increasing power of the enemy will not be effectively confronted and driven out without the power of God.

The Enemy's Strategy

Most of the cults and New Age groups are now blatantly attacking Christianity, focusing on the church as the main target of their sorcery. Not only are they infiltrating the church, but they are using their power to curse and cast spells on those in ministry. In my book, *The Harvest*, I wrote of cult members entering church meetings and performing lewd acts to intimidate and humiliate believers, and this has already begun to happen with alarming frequency.

There is a simple solution for churches that have become the target of such attacks—they must seek to know and walk in God's authority and power. He who is in us is much greater than he who is in the world (see I John 4:4). As the church grows in true spiritual authority, the cults are going to start fearing us far more than we fear them.

Sorcerers usually try to avoid direct confrontation with those who have true spiritual authority. Although they will attack those who are growing in spiritual authority and bearing fruit for the kingdom of God, this generally is not done openly but in secret. The attacks are done indirectly, by sacrificing and cursing according to the black arts.

We must recognize the power in satanic sacrifices if we are going to overcome it. In II Kings 3:27, the king of Moab offered his oldest son as a burnt offering to his demon gods, and as a result **"there came great wrath against Israel, and they departed..."** (from attacking Moab). It is not biblical for a Christian to fear the enemy, but if we do not understand and properly respect his power, we will be vulnerable to its influence.

When combating evil powers, we cannot come with carnal weapons or mere human strength; neither can we fight on Satan's terms. His first strategy in a confrontation is to get us out of the Holy Spirit's control and into a spirit of retaliation. We cannot overcome evil with evil; Satan will not cast out Satan. Jesus said, **"But if I cast out demons by the Spirit of God, then the kingdom of God has come upon you"** (Matthew 12:28).

This is why Jesus commanded us to **"bless those who curse you..."** (Luke 6:28). Blessings are more powerful than any curses, and will quickly overcome them. Even so, it is important for us to recognize when we are being cursed with witchcraft, so that we can defend against it and shine light into the darkness that has been directed against us.

Summary

Witchcraft is basically the practice of cursing others. This cursing does not just come through cults

115

or black magic arts, but can even come through those who love us and have good intentions, but are trying to manipulate us. Using manipulation or a control spirit is a form of witchcraft, regardless of who does it.

The mother who manipulates her son or daughter into marrying her choice has done it through witchcraft, and such relationships usually have to be held together through manipulation and control. The prayer group that uses prayers to expose others is gossiping for the sake of manipulation; this is not genuine prayer—it is witchcraft. Much of what is written in the name of Christian journalism, purportedly as an attempt to keep the church informed, is gossip, used to manipulate or gain influence over others. This, too, is witchcraft.

When spiritual leaders use manipulation, hype, or control to build their churches or ministries, they are operating in a counterfeit spiritual authority equivalent to witchcraft. Much of what is taught in business schools is a form of manipulation or control that is witchcraft. Many of the strategies the church has borrowed from secular journalism and the business world have brought witchcraft into the camp, and it must be removed if we are to be free to accomplish our purpose for this hour.

Many of the "yokes" and human expectations that we face have some power of manipulation and witchcraft attached to them. The enemy wants to establish these as strongholds to conflict with the calling of God in our lives. However, this is not a license to disregard the expectations of our parents, teachers, employers, etc. We were known by the Lord before we were born, and many of the influences in our lives have been placed there to help steer us toward our purpose in Him. But some of the yokes and expectations that well-intentioned parents, teachers, or coaches put on us must be cast off. When yokes are placed on us that are not from the Lord, they will become clear as we come to know our calling and purpose in Him—the truth will set us free.

The only yoke that we must take is the Lord's yoke. His yoke is easy and His burden is light (see Matthew 11:28-30). When we take His yoke, we find rest and refreshment instead of the pressure and discouragement that come even from "white" witchcraft. Pressure tactics and manipulation are subtle forms of witchcraft that can have just as much power as the black magic arts. White and black witchcraft may be different branches, but they have the same root and the same deadly poison.

Sadly, when unstable people recognize the dangers of being subject to charismatic or "white" witchcraft, they will often distort this principle in order to rebel against God's ordained authority over their lives. King Saul is a personification of one who was ordained by God but fell from his place of true spiritual authority to operate in counterfeit spiritual authority. King David, on the other hand, is a personification of true spiritual authority. How did David react to Saul? He was willing to serve in the house of Saul until Saul chased him away. Even then he never retaliated, rebelled, or tried to undermine Saul's authority, but chose instead to honor him as **"the Lord's anointed" (see I Samuel 24:10).**

We need to learn from David's example. Even though he was called to take Saul's place, he never lifted his hand against Saul. David determined that if God had really called him to be the next king, then God would have to be the one to establish him. David overcame evil with good by demonstrating the exact opposite of the manipulative or control spirits that had come against him. Had David manipulated his way into the kingdom, he would have almost certainly fallen to witchcraft, just like Saul. But David was of a different spirit.

Those who are the targets of any form of witchcraft will usually feel the sequence of stings previously listed. If we react to the attack properly, we will not only be free of its influence ourselves, but we can also help to free those who have used witchcraft. The manipulation and control spirits gain entrance through fear. Those who are fearful and insecure become so obsessed with controlling others that they use evil influence, and it will take a demonstration of **"perfect love"** to cast out these fears (see I John 4:18). Jesus commanded us to **"bless those who curse you" (see Matthew 5:44 NKJV).** Paul said that we are not to return evil for evil; we are to overcome evil with good (see Romans 12:17-21).

When we discover that we are the target of witchcraft, retaliation is not the answer. In fact, that is the very thing the enemy would have us do, for it multiplies the evil we are trying to cast out. Satan will not cast out Satan; witchcraft will not cast out witchcraft. We must pray for those who are praying against us, and bless those who are cursing us. This does not mean we are to bless what they are doing, but we must pray that they are delivered from the fears and hatred that motivate them. Pray for your attackers to have a revelation of the perfect love of God. Our greatest victory is in winning those who are in the enemy's grip, not just in afflicting them back.

There is another source of witchcraft that can be one of the most unexpected causes of our discouragement, confusion, depression, loss of vision, disorientation, and despair—ourselves! When we use manipulation, hype, or control on others, we open ourselves to the consequences. Before we look at others to find the source, we should first look at ourselves. Again, Satan cannot cast out Satan; we will not be able to cast witchcraft out of others if we are using it ourselves. Most who have been subject to witchcraft have tried to combat it in the flesh, actually using the same spirit. When we do that, it gains a foothold in our own lives that must be broken before we will have the authority to deliver others.

Witchcraft is a serious offense that God will not continue to tolerate in the church. His intent is to bring down every form and manifestation of witchcraft that has ensnared His people. After we have been freed from this terrible evil, we will also be free to walk in the unprecedented power that can only be entrusted to those who walk in true spiritual authority.

Chapter Six
The Stronghold of Illegitimate Authority

In one of the most remarkable statements made in the New Testament, Peter wrote that we should be **"looking for and hastening the coming of the day of God..." (II Peter 3:12)**. Obviously Peter would not have said this if it were not *possible* for us to hasten the coming of the day of God. But if we can hasten the coming of His day, it is apparent that we can also *delay* it. Because the enemy knows his time is short, we can be sure that he will be doing all that he can to keep us from doing what will hasten the day of the Lord, and to keep us doing that which will cause its delay.

The harvest will come. It has already come to many parts of the world, and before the end the Spirit will be poured out upon all flesh. However, there are major stumbling blocks to spiritual advancement that we must address if we are going to receive the full benefit of the impending awakening. These stumbling blocks are not big enough to stop revival altogether, but they can limit its scope, depth, duration, and fruit.

The harvest will bring the reaping of everything that has been sown, both good and evil. The harvest that marks the end of this age has already begun, but because many have the concept that the harvest is only great revival, they do not see it or understand it. The Scriptures teach that the harvest will begin with the tares being taken out first (see Matthew 13:38-40, 49), and this has been going on for some time. In many ways it seems that we have *only* been reaping tares. This may be painful for a season, but this pain will be appreciated when the full harvest begins and we are able to avoid making the same mistakes again.

One aspect of the harvest of tares that had a significant impact on the international body of Christ came with the televangelist scandals of recent years. This is not to imply that the individuals involved were "tares," but the scandals brought to light and began to uproot some erroneous practices and theologies. Unfortunately, these tares were not exposed by the church, but by the secular news media. As a friend remarked in a roundtable meeting that we hosted, "The Lord is using the secular media to discipline the church because we have refused to judge ourselves." There is an important truth to this observation.

This is by no means the first time that the Lord has used outside means to discipline His people. When Israel went astray, He would allow their heathen neighbors to conquer or oppress them. This oppression usually brought about repentance, which moved the Lord to restore Israel's sovereignty.

That the Lord is allowing the secular media to discipline the church is a loud signal announcing our fallen condition. It is likewise apparent that much of the church has sincerely given herself to repentance. A sign that this repentance has been genuine enough to be acceptable to God will be when our sovereignty is restored—when the church is able to judge herself.

Even though the Lord used the heathen nations to discipline Israel for her apostasies, He afterward would often destroy those nations for their arrogance. This may shock our human sensibilities, but those heathen nations were still heathen. They still worshipped idols, and they would inevitably try to introduce their idol worship to Israel during their occupation.

The same has been happening between the secular media and the church. Much of the Christian media has been turning to the ways of the secular media. That is not the Lord's intended means for the church's discipline, and it will result in even worse consequences if we do not rid ourselves of it.

The Wrong Kind of Repentance

Journalism has crossed a line that has made it one of the primary platforms of the **"accuser of our brethren" (see Revelation 12:10)**, and it has become a major stumbling block to spiritual advancement. This is no longer true of just secular journalism, for much of the Christian media has at times proven even less honorable and truthful in its reporting than the secular media.

Much of the Christian media is now founded more upon a humanistic philosophy of journalism than upon biblical principles. Today the Christian media is one of the greatest sources of a deadly poison that is spreading destruction in the Western church—the spirit of *unrighteous* judgment. Although it is true that the Lord had to use the media because we would not judge ourselves, the solution to that is not for us to take on the ways of the heathen, but to return to God's righteous judgment as outlined in His Word.

There is a healthy skepticism that truly *wants* to believe, such as the Bereans displayed when they searched the Scriptures to verify the message of Paul and Barnabas. However, there is another kind of skepticism that wants to *doubt*. This unhealthy form of skepticism wants to see the worst in others, because that somehow makes the skeptic feel bigger or at least feel better about his own flaws.

This kind of doubt and cynicism is both tragic and deadly. When the chronicles of this earth are read on that great judgment day, we will probably learn that this evil form of doubt was far more deadly than cancer or AIDS. Great souls rise to even greater heights by lifting others higher. Criticism has an appearance of wisdom, but it is wisdom from the dark side; it is the fruit of the Tree of the Knowledge of Good and Evil.

Since the 1960s, the news media of the West, including the Christian media, seems to have been almost completely taken over by this dark side of skepticism. It is now almost unthinkable for a Christian journalist to write an article about a church, a movement, or an event, without at least throwing in some criticism. This is often done by reporting hearsay or crude gossip as fact, without the offended parties even having been contacted for their side of the story.

Those who simply pass on gossip are just as guilty of gossiping as those who originated it. All of this is usually done in the name of "the people's right to know," or "to protect people from error." But are we really protecting them from error when we do so by committing one of the most serious errors of all— becoming stumbling blocks?

The Scriptures are shockingly honest about exposing both the good qualities and the flaws in even the greatest spiritual heroes. Yet the Bible was written as history for the sake of instructing others in the ways of God, not for the sake of exposing dirt. How does today's Christian journalism justify its departure from such biblical exhortations as these?

> **Let *no unwholesome word* proceed from your mouth, but only such a word as is good for *edification* according to the need of the moment, that it may give *grace* to those who hear (Ephesians 4:29, emphasis mine).**

And if your brother sins, go and reprove him *in private* (Matthews 18:15, emphasis mine).

The procedure for addressing sin was given to us in Matthew 18 to keep us from becoming stumbling blocks. Not following this procedure, especially in journalism, may have created more stumbling blocks to the Lord's children than any other source. Much more damage has probably come to the church by such journalism, and by so-called heresy hunting, than has come through the heresies they are trying to expose.

By What Authority?

Alexander Solzhenitsyn once said in his address at Harvard on June 8, 1978, "The press has become the greatest power within the Western countries, more powerful than the legislature, the executive and the judiciary. One would then like to ask: What law has it been elected and to whom is it responsible?" Solzhenitsyn's question is valid for Western society, but even more so for the church.

On what basis has the press been granted the extraordinary power it now has? By what authority has it been elected? The Lord appoints *elders* in the church to give it both protection and direction. He sets high standards for those elders who would be given such influence. In contrast, to whom are the Christian journalists accountable, and to what standards must they be held? These are important questions.

Just as the secular media can now manipulate public opinion and dictate policy sometimes even more effectively than our elected officials, Christian journalists can do the same in the church. Who gave them this power? Is it derived merely from an ability to be articulate or because of the anointing and commission of God? Do we have the right to have a massive influence in the church simply because we have the marketing ability to distribute our magazines, newsletters, or programs?

James warned, **"Let not many of you become teachers, my brethren, knowing that as such we shall incur a stricter judgment" (James 3:1).** It is a most serious matter to have influence in the Lord's own household! Let us be very careful how we attain it, and how we use it.

Paul explained that he did not presume to go beyond the sphere of authority that was appointed to him (see II Corinthians 10:14-18). He realized that God has given each of us certain realms of authority and grace, and we need to take care that we do not go beyond these appointed realms.

Where Are the Elders?

Much of what is done today by Christian journalism, and the heresy hunters, encroaches upon the realm of authority that was given to the elders of the church. The very meaning of the word "elder" implied a certain degree of longevity in faithful service to the church before one was given this influence. The position of elder was the highest and most respected office appointed in the biblical church.

Journalists today, on the other hand, often are not accountable to anyone but an editor. Even though they are not required to comply with any of the biblical standards for leadership in the church, they can have more influence through the media than even the most anointed true elders.

Writing can be an aspect of a biblical ministry, and there are journalists who have obvious spiritual ministries as teachers, pastors, etc. Some of these have been faithful to the biblical standards required for leaders in the church, and they should be recognized as elders in the body of Christ. For such people, journalism can be a proper platform for the authority they have been given by God. Even so, they, too, can become stumbling blocks if they do not comply with the biblical procedures for bringing correction to the church.

Most of those who are the sources of the prevailing critical spirit, or spirit of unrighteous judgment, are those who are not standing on true anointing, but on a platform of influence gained by other means. Some received their position because of professional training, which came from schools founded upon a humanistic philosophy of journalism. This philosophy does have the appearance of wisdom and the search for truth, but actually is in conflict with the Truth Himself. Others may have been given a true commission from God, but have given way to the spirit of the world.

John said, **"the whole world lies in the power of the evil one" (see I John 5:19).** The ways of the world are not the ways of God, and as Paul exhorted the Ephesians:

> **...in reference to your former manner of life, you lay aside the old self, which is being corrupted in accordance with the lusts of deceit,**
>
> **and that you be renewed in the spirit of your mind,**
>
> **and put on the new self, which in the likeness of God has been created in righteousness and holiness of the truth (Ephesians 4:22-24).**

If we're going to be **"created in righteousness and holiness of the truth,"** we must put on a new self, and live by a different philosophy than that of the world.

Good Intentions

Many Christian journalists entered the field with the intention of trying to provide an alternative source of information to the secular media. This is a noble vision and is truly needed. The church is called to be the pillar and support of the truth. However, the accuracy level of reporting in Christian journalism has not proven to be any higher than in secular journalism—it only has a more "spiritual" slant to it.

The investigative reporting done by Christian journalists on the events that I have personally witnessed, or about people that I know, has been shockingly dishonest and untrue. Some were so prone to the use of gossip, hearsay, or even apparent imagination that they could rival some of the grocery counter tabloids. Truth is our most precious commodity, and we cannot continue to allow it to be compromised, or we will receive the judgment that is promised for such deception.

Those who have been influenced by the humanistic philosophy of journalism may think we are shallow, blind, or duped if we do not expose the wrongs of others when we write about them. Yet it is much better to be ridiculed by men than it is for God to think of us as stumbling blocks.

The world's methods for seeking truth are very different from the way that real truth is found. Truth is only found in Jesus, and can only be found when we are being led by the Holy Spirit. Secular schools may be able to teach us something about the mechanics of writing or the technical knowledge needed to understand today's media tools, but the philosophy that they sow into their students has been devastating when incorporated into Christian media.

Judgment on Journalism

Christian television ministries have come under severe judgment in the past few years. Television has given some people vastly more influence in the church than God ever intended them to have. Whenever we move beyond the sphere of authority that has been appointed to us by God, we have moved beyond grace and we are bound to fall.

Other forms of Christian media are about to experience the same scrutiny that the television ministries have undergone. The Lord will ultimately deal with the secular media as well, **"For it is time for judgment to** *begin* **with the household of God..."** (**I Peter 4:17,** emphasis mine). Christian journalism will soon come under the same kind of judgment that television ministries have been experiencing.

For a period of time, the public's trust and esteem of televangelists probably sank lower than that of any other professional group, including politicians and lawyers. There are, of course, politicians and lawyers who live their lives by the highest standards of integrity, yet they still must bear the judgment of their profession. This is because there are fundamental roots in these professions that must be corrected. Likewise, there are many journalists who sincerely attempt to live by the highest standards of truth and integrity, but they are often trying to do so on a foundation that simply will not support the truth. That is why the very foundations are being shaken, so only that which cannot be shaken will remain (see Hebrews 12:25-28).

We will soon enter a period when Christian magazines, journals, newsletters, and newspapers will all come under the most intense pressure and scrutiny. The exposers are about to be exposed, and they will receive back the same measure of judgment which they measured out to others. Even those who have tried to be honest and fair, but have been operating on a humanistic foundation, will see their faulty foundation collapse.

Can this judgment be avoided? The Scriptures clearly teach that judgment can be avoided by genuine repentance. As Paul told the Corinthians, **"But if we judged ourselves rightly, we should not be judged" (I Corinthians 11:31).** Repentance is more than requesting forgiveness for our wrongs—repentance is going back to where we missed the turn and getting back on the right road. It also often includes restitution for the wrongs that have caused injury to others.

We must remember that the harvest is the reaping of what has been sown, **"For in the way you judge, you will be judged; and by your standard of measure, it will be measured to you" (Matthews 7:2).** If we have sown unrighteous judgment, then judgment will soon come upon us. If we want to reap grace, however, we should use every opportunity that we can to sow grace. If we are going to reap mercy, we must use every opportunity to sow mercy. **"Do not be deceived, God is not mocked; for whatever a man sows, this he will also reap" (Galatians 6:7).**

The Grace of True Authority

According to the many examples in the New Testament, there are times when the errors of certain movements or sects must be addressed. The Lord

Himself warned His disciples, saying, **"Beware of the leaven of the Pharisees and Sadducees" (see Matthew 16:6)**. Major portions of Galatians and other apostolic letters were devoted to correcting mistakes in doctrine or practice. The main difference between these scriptural examples, and what so often is done today, is that the biblical writers had the *authority* to bring the needed correction.

Much of the reason for so much wrong judgment—or needed correction that is given in the wrong spirit or manner—is the vacuum that exists because those who truly have been given authority by God have refrained from using it. This does not justify the wrong use of authority, or the presumption of those who try to bring correction to the church without having the authority, but it does make such actions more understandable.

We can even appreciate the courage that some have had in addressing issues that no one else would address, but that still does not make it right. Even worse, it puts those courageous people in jeopardy of becoming stumbling blocks. Paul's lament to the Corinthians still applies to the church today:

> **Or do you not know that the saints will judge the world? And if the world is judge by you, are you not competent to constitute the smallest law courts?**
>
> **Do you know that we shall judge angels? How much more, matters of this life? (I Corinthians 6:2-3)**

Possibly the main reason that the church is so full of unrighteous judgment is because there is no format for *righteous* judgment in the church. Until the elders take their proper places in the gates, churches will continue to be subject to the judgment of the secular media and heresy hunters who, regardless of how well-intentioned they may be, sow division and unrighteous judgment which wound the body of Christ more than the errors they seek to expose.

The Lord has given mandates to the church that we cannot accomplish without unity. Righteous judgment is one of them. This issue must be addressed by church leaders on every level if we are going to accomplish our mandate for this hour.

Unrighteous judgment is a source of most of the conflicts in the world. Since the church is called to be the light of this world, we should have the answers to the world's problems. How can we help to bring righteous judgment to the world if we cannot even judge ourselves?

Because of the many excesses of the past, or the tendency of some to presume authority beyond their appointed jurisdiction, it is understandable why we tend to shy away from this difficult issue. However, our continued neglect of this basic mandate to provide righteous judgment will prove increasingly costly. Until we bring proper judgment to the church, and then through the church to our society, we will continue to be subject to the unrighteous judgment of the world.

Part III

THE RELIGIOUS SPIRIT

Chapter Seven

Combating the Religious Spirit

Loving God is the greatest commandment, and the greatest gift that we can possess. The second great commandment is to love our neighbor. As the Lord affirmed, the whole Law is fulfilled by keeping these two commandments. That is, if we keep these two commandments, we will keep the whole Law (see Matthew 22:34-40, Romans 13:8).

If we love the Lord, we will not worship idols. If we love our neighbors, we will not envy them, steal from them, murder them, etc. Therefore, keeping these two positive commandments to love will enable us to fulfill all of the negative "do nots" of the Law.

Simple love for God will overcome most of the evil in our hearts, and it is the most powerful weapon against evil in the world. Because loving God is our highest goal, it must be the primary focus of our lives. That is why one of the enemy's most deceptive and deadly attacks upon the church is meant to divert us from this ultimate quest. It is his strategy to keep us focused on the evil in our lives, knowing that we will become what we are beholding (see II Corinthians 3:18). As long as we keep looking at the evil, it will continue to have dominion over us. When we look to the Lord and behold His glory, we will be changed into His image.

This is not to imply that we should ignore the sins and errors that are in our lives. In fact, the Scriptures command us to examine and test ourselves to be sure that we are still in the faith (see II Corinthians 13:5). The issue is what we do after the iniquity is discovered. Do we turn to the Tree of the Knowledge of Good and Evil, or to the Tree of Life? Do we try to make ourselves better so that we will then be acceptable to God, or do we turn to the cross of Jesus to find both the forgiveness and the power to overcome the sin?

A primary strategy of the enemy is intended to keep us focused on the evil, partaking of the Tree of Knowledge, and away from the glory of the Lord and the cross. This tactic comes in the form of a religious spirit, an evil spirit that is the counterfeit of the true love of God and true worship. It has probably done far more damage to the church than the New Age movement and all other cults combined.

The Nature of a Religious Spirit

A religious spirit is a demon which seeks to substitute religious activity for the power of the Holy

Spirit in our lives. Its primary objective is to have the church "**holding to a form of godliness, although they have denied its power**" (**II Timothy 3:5**). The Apostle Paul completed his exhortation with "**avoid such men as these.**" This religious spirit is the "**...leaven of the Pharisees and Sadducees**" (**Matthew 16:6**) of which the Lord warned His disciples to beware.

The Lord often used metaphors to illustrate the lessons He taught. The religious spirit does operate like the leaven in bread. It does not add substance or nutritional value to the bread, it only inflates it. Such is the by-product of the religious spirit. It does not add to the life and power of the church, but merely feeds the very pride of man which caused the first Fall, and almost every fall since.

Satan seems to understand even better than the church that "**God resists the proud, but gives grace to the humble**" (**James 4:6** NKJV). He knows very well that God will not inhabit any work that is inflated with pride, and that God Himself will even resist such a work. So Satan's strategy is to make us proud— even proud of good things, such as how much we read our Bibles, or witness, or feed the poor. He knows that if we do the will of God in pride, our work will be counterproductive and could even ultimately work toward our fall.

Satan also knows that once leaven gets into the bread, it is extremely difficult to remove. Pride, by its very nature, is the most difficult stronghold to remove or correct. A religious spirit keeps us from hearing the voice of God by encouraging us to assume that we already know God's opinion, what He is saying, and what pleases Him. This delusion is the result of believing that God is just like us. This will even cause the rationalization of Scripture, having us believe that rebukes, exhortations, and words of correction are for other people, but not for us.

If a religious spirit is a problem in your life, you have probably already begun to think about how badly someone you know needs to read this message. It may not even have occurred to you that God put this into your hands because you need it. In fact, we all need it. This is one enemy that all of us are probably battling to some degree. It is imperative that we get free of this devastating deception, and stay free. We will not be able to worship the Lord in Spirit and truth until we do.

The degree to which we have been delivered from this powerful deception will directly affect the degree to which we will be able to preach the true gospel in power. The church's confrontation with the religious spirit will be one of the epic battles of the last days. Everyone will be fighting in this battle. The only issue to be determined is which side we will be on.

We will not have the authority to deliver others from darkness if we are not free from it ourselves. To begin taking ground from this vast enemy, we must ask the Lord to shine His light on us, showing how this applies to us personally. As illustrated by the

Lord's continual confrontations with the Pharisees, the church's most desperate fight from the very beginning has been with this spirit. Just as the primary characteristic of the Pharisees was focusing on what was wrong with others while being blind to their own faults, the religious spirit tries to make us do the same.

The Great Deception

One of the most deceptive characteristics about the religious spirit is that it is founded upon zeal for God. We tend to think that zeal for God cannot be evil, but that depends on why we are zealous for Him.

Paul wrote of his Jewish brethren in Romans 10:2: **"For I bear them witness that they have a zeal for God, but not in accordance with knowledge."** No one on earth prayed more, fasted more, read the Bible more, had a greater hope in the coming of the Messiah, or had more zeal for the things of God than the Pharisees. Yet, they were the greatest opposers of God and His Messiah when He came.

The young Saul of Tarsus was motivated by zeal for God while he was persecuting His church. Zeal for God is one of the most desperately needed characteristics of the church today, most of which is bound by a terrible Laodicean lukewarmness. The Lord commanded the Laodicean church to **"...be zealous therefore, and repent" (Revelation 3:19)**.

Those who are truly zealous are the most difficult to stop, so the enemy's strategy against them is to push them too far. His first step is to get them to glory in their own zeal. Regardless of how important a gift or characteristic is that we have, if the enemy can get us to take pride in it, he will have us in his snare and will use that gift for evil.

The Lord had little trouble with demons while He walked the earth. They quickly recognized His authority and begged for mercy. It was the conservative, zealous, religious community that immediately became His greatest enemy. Those who were the most zealous for the Word of God crucified the Word Himself when He became flesh to walk among them. The same is still true.

All of the cults and false religions combined have not done as much damage to the moves of God as the opposition, or infiltration, of the religious spirit in the church. Cults and false religions are easily discerned, but the religious spirit has thwarted or diverted possibly every revival or movement to date, and it still retains a seat of honor throughout most of the visible church.

It is a manifestation of the religious spirit that will take its seat in the very temple of God, declaring himself to be God (see II Thessalonians 2:4). The temple of God is no longer made with hands, and this is not speaking about a building in Jerusalem. This man of sin will take his seat in the church. Unfortunately, it will be the church that allows him to do this.

The Two Foundations

Like most of the enemy's strongholds, the religious spirit builds its work on two basic foundations: fear and pride. The religious spirit seeks to have us serve the Lord in order to gain His approval, rather than from a position of having received our approval through the cross of Jesus. Therefore, the religious spirit bases relationship to God on personal discipline rather than the propitiatory sacrifice of Christ. The motivation for doing this can be either fear or pride, or a combination of both.

Fear and pride are the two basic results of the Fall, and our deliverance from them is usually a long process. That is why the Lord even gave Jezebel "time to repent" (see Revelation 2:20-21). The biblical Jezebel, the wife of King Ahab, was a very religious woman, but she was given to false religion. The Lord gave her time to repent, because the roots of this spirit go so deep that time is required to fully repent and be delivered from it.

However, even though the Lord gave Jezebel time to repent, He rebuked the church of Thyatira for tolerating her (verse 20). We can be patient with people who have religious spirits, but we must not tolerate their ministry in our midst while we are waiting! If this spirit is not confronted quickly, it will possibly do more damage to the church, our ministries, our families, and our lives, than any other assault that we may suffer.

The Foundation of Guilt

Eli, the priest who raised Samuel, is a biblical example of someone who ministered in a religious spirit founded upon guilt. Eli had so much zeal for the Lord that when he heard that the ark had been captured by the Philistines, he fell over and died. He had spent his life trying to serve the Lord as the high priest, but the very first prophetic word given to Samuel was one of the most frightening rebukes given in the Scriptures—and it was directed to Eli!

"For I have told him that I am about to judge his house forever for the iniquity which he knew, because his sons brought a curse on themselves and he did not rebuke them.

"And therefore I have sworn to the house of Eli that the iniquity of Eli's house shall not be atoned for by sacrifice or offering forever" (I Samuel 3:13-14).

Eli's zeal for the Lord was based on sacrifices and offerings intended to compensate for his irresponsibility as a father. Guilt can spur us on to great zeal for the Lord, and our sacrifices and offerings become an attempt to atone for our failures. This is an affront to the cross, which alone can atone for our guilt. Such zeal will never be acceptable to the Lord, even if we could make sacrifices forever.

We should note here that the Lord never said that Eli's sin couldn't be forgiven. He just said that Eli's attempts to atone for sin by sacrifice and offering would never succeed. There are multitudes of men and women whose zeal for the Lord is likewise based on an attempt to atone for sin, failure, or irresponsibility in other areas of their lives. But all the sacrifices in the world will not atone for even our smallest failure. To even make such an attempt is an insult to the cross of Jesus, which is the only acceptable sacrifice to the Father for sin.

Attempting to gain God's approval by our own sacrifice opens the door wide for a religious spirit, because such service is not based on the blood of Jesus, but on an attempt to make our own atonement for sin. This doesn't mean we should not do things to please the Lord, but we must keep as our motive to be pleasing to the Lord for His joy, not for our acceptance. One is God-centered; the other is self-centered. And this is self-centeredness of the most destructive kind—an attempt to circumvent the cross.

It is also noteworthy that one of the sins of Eli's sons was that they "... **despised the offering of the Lord**" **(I Samuel 2:17)**. They appropriated for their own selfish use the sacrifices and offerings brought to the Lord. Those who are gripped by this form of a religious spirit will often be the most zealous to preach the cross, but herein lies the perversion: It emphasizes their cross more than the cross of Jesus. Their delight really is more in self-abasement than in the cross of Christ, which alone makes us righteous and acceptable to God.

The Foundation of Pride

Idealism is one of the most deceptive and destructive disguises of the religious spirit. Idealism is of human origin, and is a form of humanism. Although it has the appearance of seeking only the highest standards and the preservation of God's glory, idealism is possibly the most deadly enemy of true revelation and true grace. It is deadly because it does not allow for growing up into grace and wisdom, but attacks and destroys the foundation of those who are in pursuit of God's glory, but are not yet there.

Idealism makes us try to impose on others standards that are beyond what God has required or given the grace for at that time. For example, men controlled by this kind of religious spirit may condemn those who are not praying two hours a day as they are. The truth is, it may be God's will for us to be praying that much, but how we get there is crucial. The grace of God may first call us to pray just ten minutes a day. Then, as we become so blessed by His presence, we will want to spend more and more time with Him until we will not want to quit after ten minutes, then an hour, then two. When we eventually are praying two hours a day, it will be because of our love for prayer and the presence of the Lord, not out of fear or pride.

A person with a religious spirit based on idealism will usually seek the perfect church, and will refuse to be a part of anything less. Those led by the Holy Spirit may also have high hopes for a church, but will still be able to give themselves in service to even some of the lowliest works, in order to help those works grow in vision and maturity. The Holy Spirit is called **"the Helper"** (see John 14:26), and those who are truly led by the Spirit will always be looking for ways to help, not just to stand aloof and criticize.

When a religious spirit is founded upon pride, it is evidenced by perfectionism. The perfectionist sees everything as black or white. This develops into extremes, requiring that every person and every teaching be judged as either 100 percent right or 100 percent wrong. This is a standard with which only Jesus could comply; it will lead to a serious delusion when we impose it on ourselves or others. True grace imparts a truth that sets people free, showing them the way out of their sin, and beckoning them to higher levels of spiritual maturity.

One with a religious spirit can usually point to problems with great accuracy, but seldom has solutions, except to tear down what has already been built. This is the strategy of the enemy to nullify progress that is being made, and to sow a discouragement that will limit future progress. This produces the mentality that, if we cannot go straight to the top of the mountain, we should not climb at all, but just "die to self." This is a death that God has not required, and it is a perversion of the exhortation for us to take up our crosses daily.

The perfectionist both imposes and tries to live by standards that stifle true maturity and growth. The grace of God will lead us up the mountain step-by-step. The Lord does not condemn us because we may trip a few times while trying to climb. He graciously picks us up with encouragement that we can make it. We must have a vision of making it to the top, and should never condemn ourselves for not being there yet, as long as we are still climbing.

James said, **"For we all stumble in many ways" (James 3:2)**. If we had to wait until we were perfect before we could minister, no one would ever qualify for the ministry. Even though perfect obedience and understanding should always be our goal, such will never be found within ourselves, but only as we come to perfectly abide in the Perfect One.

Because we now **"see through a glass darkly" (see I Corinthians 13:12 KJV)**, or in part, we must always be open to greater accuracy in our beliefs and teachings. One of the greatest delusions is that we are already complete in our understanding, or 100 percent accurate in our perceptions or actions. Those with a religious spirit will usually claim to be open to more understanding, but most of the time this is done to get everyone else to be open to what they teach, while they remain steadfastly closed to others.

Jesus blessed Peter and turned the keys of the kingdom over to him just before He had to rebuke him by calling him "Satan" (see Matthew 16:23). Right after this greatest of blessings, the enemy deceived him, yet the Lord did not take the keys away from Peter! In fact, Jesus knew when He gave the keys to Peter that he was soon to deny even knowing Him.

Many years after Peter used the keys to open the door of faith for both the Jews and Gentiles, **"the least of the apostles,"** Paul, had to rebuke him publicly because of his hypocrisy (see I Corinthians 15:9, Galatians 2:11-14). Even so, Peter was promised that he would sit on one of the twelve thrones judging the twelve tribes of Israel (see Matthew 19:28). The Lord has proven that He will commission and use men long before most of us would, and when He calls us, He already knows all the mistakes that we will make.

It seems that the Lord's leadership style was to provide a place where His followers could make mistakes and learn from them. If we required our children to be perfectly mature while they were still children, it would stifle their growth and maturity. The same is true in the church. We must correct mistakes, because that is how we learn, but it must be a correction that encourages and frees, not one that condemns and crushes initiative.

The Deadly Combination

One of the most powerful and deceptive forms of the religious spirit is built upon the foundations of both fear and pride. Those who are bound in this way go through periods of deep anguish and remorse at their failures, but this false repentance results only in more self-abasement, and further attempts to make sacrifices that will appease the Lord. Those bound by a religious spirit often flip to the other side, where they become so convinced that they are superior to other Christians or other groups that they become unteachable and unable to receive reproof. The foundation that they stand on at any given time will be dictated more by external pressure than by true conviction.

Such a religious spirit is so slippery that it will wiggle out of almost any attempt to confront it. If you address the pride, the fears and insecurities will rise up to attract sympathy. If you confront the fear, it will then change into religious pride masquerading as faith. This type of spirit will drive individuals or congregations to such extremes that they will inevitably disintegrate.

The Counterfeit Gift of Discernment

A religious spirit will usually give a counterfeit gift of discernment of spirits. This counterfeit gift thrives on seeing what is wrong with others rather than seeing what God is doing so we can help them along. This is how a religious spirit does some of its greatest damage to the church. Its ministry will almost always leave more damage and division than healing and reconciliation. Its wisdom is rooted in the Tree of the Knowledge of Good and Evil, and though the truth may be accurate, it is ministered in a spirit that kills.

This counterfeit gift of discernment is motivated by suspicion and fear. The suspicion is rooted in such things as rejection, territorial preservation, or general insecurity. The true gift of discernment can only function through love. Any motive other than love will distort spiritual perception. Whenever someone submits a judgment or criticism about another person or group, we should disregard it unless we know that the one bringing it truly loves that person or group, and has an "investment" of service to them.

Angels of Light

When Paul warned the Corinthians about those who ministered in a religious spirit, which sought to bring a yoke of legalism upon the young church, he explained that:

> **For such men are false apostles, deceitful workers, disguising themselves as apostles of Christ.**

> **And no wonder, for even Satan disguises himself as an angel of light.**

> **Therefore it is not surprising if his servants also disguise themselves as servants of righteousness…(II Corinthians 11:13-15).**

This phrase **"angel of light"** could be interpreted as a "messenger of truth." Satan's most deceptive and deadly disguise is to come as a servant of righteousness, using truths for the purpose of destruction. He is quite skillful at quoting Scripture and using wisdom, but it is the wisdom of the Tree of Knowledge—wisdom that kills. He can accurately point out what is wrong with someone else, but he always does it in such a way that tears down, not offering solutions that lead to deliverance and life.

"Angels of light," who are empowered by a religious spirit, will first look for what is wrong with someone rather than for what is right. Although this spirit usually comes in the guise of protecting the sheep, the truth, or the Lord's glory, it is an evil, critical spirit that will always end up causing division and destruction.

Criticism gives an appearance of wisdom, but it is pride in one of its most base forms. When we criticize someone, we are in effect declaring ourselves to be better than them. We may be better than others in some areas, but if we are, it is only by grace. Believers who recognize the true grace of God never look for ways to put others down, but rather find ways to build them up. As an old proverb declares, "Any jackass can kick a barn down, but it requires a skillful carpenter to build one."

The Religious Spirit and Murder

When Adam and Eve chose to live by the Tree of the Knowledge of Good and Evil, they were partaking of the religious spirit. The first result of this was self-centeredness—they started looking at themselves. The first child born to them after partaking of this fruit was Cain, who is the first biblical model of a man controlled by the religious spirit.

Cain was **"a tiller of the ground" (see Genesis 4:2),** or earthly minded. The religious spirit will always seek to keep us focused on the earthly realm rather than the heavenly realm. This "seed of Cain" judges by what is seen and cannot understand those who **"endured, as seeing Him who is unseen" (see Hebrews 11:27).**

In Revelation 13:11, we see the second beast **"coming up out of the earth."** This is because the spiritual seed of Cain are tillers of the ground. This earthly-mindedness has produced one of the most evil beasts the world will ever know.

Cain also tried to make an offering to the Lord from his own labors. God rejected that sacrifice, but accepted Abel's sacrifice of blood. The fruit of our labors will never be an acceptable offering to the Lord. This was a statement from the beginning that God would only accept the blood of the Lamb. Instead of receiving this correction and repenting, Cain became jealous of his brother and killed him. Those who attempt to live by their own works will often become enraged at those who take their stand on the righteousness of the Lamb.

That is why Saul of Tarsus, the Pharisee of Pharisees, was so enraged against Christians. They represented the greatest threat to that which the Pharisees had built their whole lives upon. Because of this, the Pharisees could not endure the very existence of the Christians. Religions that are based on works will easily become violent. This includes "Christian" sects where a doctrine of works has supplanted the cross of Christ.

The Lord said that if a man hates his brother, he is guilty of murder (see Matthew 5:21-22). Those who are driven by religious spirits may well try to destroy people by means other than the physical taking of their lives. Many of the onslaughts of slander instigated against churches and ministries are the ragings of this same religious spirit that caused Cain to slay his brother.

The Test of a True Messenger

In Ezekiel 37, the prophet was taken to a valley full of dry bones and asked if they could live. The Lord then commanded him to "prophesy to the bones." As he prophesied, they came together, came to life, and then became a great army.

This is an important test which every true ministry must pass. The true prophet can see a great army in even the driest of bones. He will prophesy life to those bones until they come to life and then become an army. A false prophet with a religious spirit will do little more than just tell the bones how dry they are, heaping discouragement and condemnation on them, but imparting no life or power to overcome their circumstances.

Apostles and prophets are given authority to build up and tear down, but we have no right to tear down if we have not first built up. We should give no one the authority to bring correction to the people under our care unless they first have a history of providing spiritual nourishment and building people up. Some may say that such a policy would eliminate the ministry of the prophets altogether, but I say that so-called "prophets" who do not have a heart to build people up should be eliminated from ministry. As Jude said of them, **"These men are grumblers and faultfinders" (see Jude 16 NIV)** who are **"hidden reefs in your love feasts" (see Jude 12).**

Even so, as we can see from Eli's tragic example, woe to the shepherds who feed and care for the sheep, but fail to correct them. The true grace of God is found between the extremes of unrighteous faultfinding and unsanctified mercy (approving of things that God condemns). Either extreme can be the result of a religious spirit.

Chapter Eight

The Spirit of Jezebel

The spirit of Jezebel is a form of the religious spirit. Just as Jezebel was the ambitious and manipulative wife of King Ahab—a weak leader who allowed her to dictate policy in his kingdom— the Jezebel spirit will usually be found supplanting weak leadership. The Jezebel spirit usually gains its dominion by making political alliances, and often it uses a deceptively humble and submissive demeanor in order to manipulate. However, once this spirit gains authority, it will usually manifest a strong control spirit and shameless presumption. Despite its name, this spiritual problem is not limited to women.

Jezebel **"calls herself a prophetess" (see Revelation 2:20).** This is often one of the telltale signs of false prophets who are operating in a religious spirit—they are preoccupied with their own recognition. To the degree that self-seeking and the need for recognition abide within us, our ministry will be corrupted. Those who are easily offended because they are not given an important title or position should never be accepted by that title or given that position! The difference between those motivated by a desire for recognition and those motivated by love for the Lord is the difference between the false prophet and the true. The Lord Himself declared:

> **He who speaks from himself seeks his own glory** [literally: "recognition"]**; but He who is seeking the glory of the one who sent Him, He is true, and there is no unrighteousness in Him (John 7:18).**

Demanding recognition for herself, Jezebel serves as the enemy of the true prophetic ministry. Jezebel was the greatest enemy of one of the Old Covenant's most powerful prophets, Elijah, whose ministry especially typified preparing the way for the Lord. The Jezebel spirit is one of the most potent forms of the religious spirit, which seeks to keep the church and the world from being prepared for the return of the Lord.

The Jezebel spirit especially attacks the prophetic ministry, because that ministry has an important place in preparing the way for the Lord. That is why John the Baptist was persecuted by a personification of Jezebel, in the wife of Herod. The prophetic ministry is the primary vehicle through which the Lord gives timely, strategic direction to His people. Jezebel knows that removing the true prophets will make the people vulnerable to her false prophets, always resulting in idolatry and spiritual adultery.

When there is a void of hearing the true voice of the Lord, the people will be much more susceptible to the deceptions of the enemy. This is why Jesus called the religious leaders of His own day **"blind guides" (see Matthew 23:16).** These men, who knew the messianic prophecies better than anyone else in the world, looked into the face of the One who perfectly fulfilled those prophecies and thought that He was sent from Beelzebub.

Jezebel's prophets of Baal were also given to sacrifice, even to the point of cutting and flailing themselves while seeking the manifestation of their god. A primary strategy of the religious spirit is to get the church devoted to "sacrifice" in a way that perverts the command for us to take up our crosses daily. This perversion will have us putting more faith in our sacrifices than in the Lord's sacrifice. It will also use sacrifices and offerings to pressure God to manifest Himself. This is a form of the terrible delusion that we can somehow purchase the grace and presence of God with our good works.

The Root of Self-Righteousness

We do not crucify ourselves for the sake of righteousness, purification, spiritual maturity, or to get the Lord to manifest Himself; this is nothing less than conjuring. We are **"crucified with Christ"** (see

Galatians 2:20). If we "crucify ourselves," it will only result in self-righteousness—which is pride in one of its most base forms. This pride is deceptive, because it gives the appearance of wisdom and righteousness, of which the Apostle Paul warned:

> **Let no one keep defrauding you of your prize by delighting in self-abasement and the worship of the angels, taking his stand on visions he has seen, inflated without cause by his fleshly mind,**

> **and not holding fast to the head, from whom the entire body, being supplied and held together by the joints and ligaments, grows with a growth which is from God.**

> **If you have died with Christ to the elementary principles of the world, why, as if you were living in the world, do you submit yourself to decrees, such as,**

> **"Do not handle, do not taste, do not touch!"**

> **(which all refer to things destined to perish with the using)—in accordance with the commandments and teachings of men?**

> **These are matters which have, to be sure, the appearance of wisdom in self-made religion and self-abasement and severe treatment of the body, but are of no value**

against fleshly indulgence (**Colossians 2:18-23**).

The religious spirit will make us feel very good about our spiritual condition as long as it is self-centered and self-seeking. Pride feels good; it can even be exhilarating. But it keeps all of our attention on how well we are doing and on how we stand compared to others—not on the glory of God. This results in our putting confidence in discipline and personal sacrifice rather than in the Lord and His sacrifice.

Of course, discipline and a commitment to self-sacrifice are essential qualities for every believer to have. But it is the motivation behind them that determines whether we are being driven by a religious spirit or by the Holy Spirit. A religious spirit motivates through fear and guilt, or through pride and ambition. The motivation of the Holy Spirit is love for the Son of God.

Delighting in self-abasement is a sure symptom of the religious spirit. This does not mean that we can neglect to discipline ourselves, fast, or buffet our bodies as Paul did. However, the problem comes when we take a perverse delight in this, rather than delighting in the Son of God.

Deceptive Revelation

Colossians 2:18-19 indicates that a person with a religious spirit will tend to delight in self-abasement and will often be given to worshiping angels or taking improper stands on visions he has seen. A religious spirit wants us to worship anything or anyone but Jesus. The same spirit that is given to worshiping angels will also be prone to excessively exalting people. We must beware of anyone who unduly exalts angels, or men and women of God, or anyone who uses the visions he has received in order to gain improper influence in the church. God does not give us revelations so that people will respect us more, or to prove our ministry. The fruit of true revelation will be humility, not pride.

Of course, the Scriptures teach that Christians do have these prophetic experiences, and we are also told in Acts 2:17 that they will increase in the last days. Jesus also warned that in the last days there would be many false prophets (see Matthew 24:11). Prophetic revelation that is truly from God is crucial to the body of Christ. The enemy knows this very well, which is why he will raise up many false prophets. But they can be easily discerned. As Paul warned the Colossians, the danger doesn't come from those who are having prophetic revelations, but from those who have been inflated by them.

A religious spirit will always feed our fear or pride, whereas genuine spiritual maturity will always lead to increasing humility. This progression of humility is wonderfully demonstrated in the life of Paul the Apostle. In his letter to the Galatians, estimated to have been written in 56 A.D., he declared that when he visited the original apostles in Jerusalem, they "**...contributed nothing to me**" (see **Galatians 2:6**). He was by this declaring that he had as much as they did.

In Paul's first letter to the Corinthians, written about six years later, he called himself the "**least of the apostles**" (see **I Corinthians 15:9**). In Ephesians 3:8, written in about 61 A.D., he declared himself to be the "**...the very least of all saints.**" When writing to Timothy in approximately 65 A.D., Paul declared himself to be the "**foremost of all sinners**" (see **I Timothy 1:15**), adding that he had found mercy. A true revelation of God's mercy is a great antidote for the religious spirit. It is clear by this that the great apostle was not completely free of pride in the first years of his ministry. Which of us can claim to be free of it either? However, we are all hopefully growing in grace and, therefore, humility.

Young apostles may exude a lot of pride, but they can still be true apostles. The key here is in which direction we are going. Are we being puffed up by our revelations, our commission, or our accomplishments? Or are we growing in grace and humility?

The Martyr Syndrome

When combined with the religious spirit, the martyr syndrome is one of the ultimate and most deadly delusions. To be true martyrs for the faith and literally lose our lives for the sake of Christ is one of the greatest honors that we can receive in this life. Yet, when this is perverted, it is a most tragic form of deception.

When a religious spirit is combined with the martyr syndrome, it is almost impossible for that person to be delivered from the deception that he is "suffering for the gospel." At this point, any rejection or correction received from others is perceived as the price he must pay to "stand for the truth." This warped perspective will drive him even further from the truth and any possibility of correction.

The martyr syndrome can also be a manifestation of the spirit of suicide. It is sometimes easier to "die for the Lord" than it is to live for Him. Those who have a perverted understanding of the cross glory more in death than they do in life. They fail to see that the point of the cross is the resurrection, not the grave.

Self-Help Psychology

There is a "self-help psychology" movement that is attempting to replace the power of the cross in the church. Humanistically-based psychology is "a different gospel" (see II Corinthians 11:4); it is an enemy of the cross, and is another form of the religious spirit. Paul warned us:

> As you therefore have received Christ Jesus the Lord, so walk in Him,
>
> having been firmly rooted and now being built up in Him, and established in your faith, just as you were instructed, and overflowing with gratitude.

> **See to it that no one takes you captive through philosophy and empty deception, according to the tradition of men, according to the elementary principles of the world, rather than according to Christ (Colossians 2:6-8).**

We all need "inner healing" to some degree, but much of what is being called inner healing is nothing less than digging up the "old man" and trying to get him healed. The answer to these deep wounds is not a procedure or a formula, but simple forgiveness. When we go to the cross and find forgiveness and true acceptance based on the blood of Jesus, we will find a perfect love able to cast out all of our fears and wash away all bitterness and resentment.

This seems too simple, but that is why Paul said: **"But I am afraid, lest as the serpent deceived Eve by his craftiness, your minds should be led astray from the simplicity and purity of devotion to Christ" (II Corinthians 11:3).** Salvation is simple. Deliverance is simple. Yet there is a major strategy of the enemy to dilute the power of the gospel by having us add to it, which is how Eve was deceived. We add to it because we just do not think it will be acceptable unless it somehow seems brilliant or abstract. That is precisely why we must become like children to enter the kingdom.

The Lord commanded the man and woman not to eat from the Tree of the Knowledge of Good and

Evil because they would die. When the serpent asked about this command, Eve replied that they could not eat from the tree **"or touch it" (see Genesis 3:3).** However, the Lord had not said anything about refraining from touching the tree. Adding to God's commandments is just as destructive as taking away from them. Anyone who thinks that he can so flippantly add to the Word of God does not respect it enough to keep it when the testing comes. If Satan can get us to either add or subtract from the Word, he then knows our fall is imminent, just like it was for Eve.

Although there are many "Christian" philosophies and therapies that seem wise, most are in fact attempting to be substitutes for the Holy Spirit in our lives. Some people do need counseling, and there are outstanding Christian counselors who do lead people to the cross. But others are simply leading people into a black hole of self-centeredness that will consume them and try to suck in everyone else around them, too. In spite of the Christian terminology, this philosophy is an enemy of the cross of Christ.

Summary

Basically, the religious spirit seeks to replace the Holy Spirit as the source of spiritual life. It does this by seeking to replace true repentance, which leads to grace, with a repentance based on our performance. The effect of this is to replace true humility with pride.

True religion is based on loving the Lord and then loving our neighbors. True religion will promote discipline and obedience, but these are founded on love for the Lord rather than the need or desire for recognition or acceptance. The wife who keeps herself in shape because she loves her husband will be easily distinguished from the one who does it because of her own ego. The former will carry her beauty with grace and dignity; the latter may be physically appealing, but it will be a seductive appeal that is a perversion of true love.

The religious spirit is basically a manifestation of the "good" side of the Tree of the Knowledge of Good and Evil. When Adam and Eve ate of that tree in the Garden, the first result was that they looked at themselves. Self-centeredness is the poison that made that fruit deadly, and it is still the most deadly poison the serpent seeks to give us. In contrast with the religious spirit—which causes us to focus our attention on ourselves and base our concept of the Christian life on performance—the Holy Spirit will always lead us into a life that is Christ-centered.

The Holy Spirit produces fruit by joining us to the Lord and applying the work He accomplished for us on the cross: **"For the word of the cross is to those who are perishing foolishness, but to us who are being saved it is the power of God" (I Corinthians 1:18).** However, we must understand that this is the cross of Christ, not our own cross. We are called to deny ourselves and take up our crosses daily, but we are not to glory in self-abasement or try to live by the virtue of our own sacrifices. Rather, we are to glory in what Jesus accomplished and the sacrifice that He made (see Philippians 3:3).

We have our standing before God solely on the basis of the cross of Christ. Our ability to come boldly before the throne of God has nothing to do with whether we have had a good or a bad day, or how properly we have performed all of our religious duties. Our acceptance before God and our ability to come into His presence is based on one thing only—the sacrifice that Jesus made for our justification.

This does not negate the need for personal holiness. As James asserted, **"Even so, faith, if it has no works, is dead..." (James 2:17).** If we are joined to Christ, we will not go on living in sin. However, we do not become free from sin in order to abide in Him, but by abiding in Him. Jesus is the Way, the Truth, and the Life. If He is not our Life, then we do not really know the Way or the Truth either. It is the religious spirit that tries to keep Christianity in the realm of the Way and the Truth, while keeping us from the essential union by which Jesus becomes our Life. True Christianity involves not just what we believe, but Whom we believe.

True worship does not have as its purpose to see the Lord; rather, worship comes from having seen Him. When we see Him, we will worship. When we see His glory, we will no longer be captivated by our own positive or negative qualities; our souls will be captured by His beauty. When the Lamb enters, even the twenty-four elders will cast their crowns at His feet (see Revelation 4:10). That is the goal of true faith—to see Him, to abide in Him, and to reveal Him.

The world is becoming increasingly repulsed by religion. However, when Jesus is lifted up, all men will be drawn to Him (see John 12:32). Because the whole creation was created through Him and for Him, we all have a Jesus-size hole in our soul. Nothing else will ever satisfy the longing of the human heart or bring us peace, except a genuine relationship with Christ Jesus.

When we are truly joined to Jesus, unstoppable living waters begin to flow out of our innermost being. As more and more people are freed and this water begins to flow in them, it will become a great river of life in the midst of the earth. Those who drink from this river will never thirst again—they will have found satisfaction for the deepest yearning of the human soul. The more that we get free of the religious spirit, the purer and clearer these waters will be.

Chapter Nine

The Warning Signs
of the Religious Spirit

The following is a list of some of the more obvious warning signs of the religious spirit. As stated, almost everyone is battling the religious spirit to at least some degree, and everyone's fight is somewhat different. One may be dealing with all the issues listed below to a small degree, and yet be more free from the yoke of the religious spirit than one who is free of most of these problems, but who has serious problems with just a couple of them.

Our goal must be to get completely free of any influence from the religious spirit by being completely submitted to the Holy Spirit. Without this complete submission to the Lord, there is no way to be free from the religious spirit.

People with a religious spirit:

1. Will often see their primary mission as the tearing down of whatever they believe is wrong. Such

a person's ministry will result more in division and destruction than in lasting works that are bearing fruit for the kingdom.

2. Will be unable to accept a rebuke, especially from those they judge to be less spiritual than themselves. Think back on how you responded the last few times someone tried to correct you.

3. Will have a philosophy that, "I will not listen to people, but only to God." Since God frequently speaks through people, this is an obvious delusion, revealing serious spiritual pride.

4. Will be inclined to see more of what is wrong with other people, other churches, etc., than what is right with them. From the valley John saw Babylon, but when he was carried to a high mountain, he saw the New Jerusalem (see Revelation 21:10). If we are only seeing Babylon, it is because of our perspective. Those who are in a place of true vision will have their attention on what God is doing, not men.

5. Will be subject to an overwhelming feeling of guilt that they can never measure up to the Lord's standards. This is a root of the religious spirit because it causes us to base our relationship with Him on our performance rather than on the cross. Jesus has already measured up for us; He is the completed work that the Father is seeking to accomplish within us. Our whole goal in life should be simply to abide in Him.

6. Will keep score on their spiritual lives. This includes feeling better about ourselves because we go

to more meetings, read our Bibles more, do more things for the Lord, etc. These are all noble endeavors, but the true measure of spiritual maturity is getting closer to the Lord.

7. Will believe that they have been appointed to fix everyone else. These persons become the self-appointed watchmen, or sheriffs, in God's kingdom. They are seldom involved in building, but serve only to keep the church in a state of annoyance and agitation, if not causing serious divisions.

8. Will have a leadership style which is bossy, overbearing, and intolerant of the weakness or failure of others. James said: **"But the wisdom from above is first pure, then peaceable, gentle, reasonable, full of mercy and good fruits, unwavering, without hypocrisy. And the seed whose fruit is righteousness is sown in peace by those who make peace" (James 3:17-18).**

9. Will have a sense that they are closer to God than other people, or that their lives or ministries are more pleasing to Him. This is a symptom of the profound delusion that we draw closer to God because of who we are, rather than through Jesus.

10. Will take pride in their spiritual maturity and discipline, especially as compared to others. True spiritual maturity involves growing up into Christ. When we begin to compare ourselves to others, it is obvious that we have lost sight of the true goal—Jesus.

11. Will believe that they are on the "cutting edge" of what God is doing. This includes thinking

that we are involved in the most important thing that God is doing.

12. Will have a mechanical prayer life. When we start feeling relief when our prayer time is over or we have prayed through our prayer list, we should consider our condition. We will never feel relief when our conversations are over with the one we love.

13. Will do things in order to be noticed by people. This is a symptom of the idolatry of fearing people more than we fear God, which results in a religion that serves men instead of God.

14. Will be overly repulsed by emotionalism. When people who are subject to a religious spirit encounter the true life of God, it will usually appear to them to be excessive, emotional, and carnal. True passion for God is often emotional and demonstrative, such as David exemplified when he brought the ark of God into Jerusalem (see II Samuel 6:14-16).

15. Will use emotionalism as a substitute for the work of the Holy Spirit. This seems contradictory to the previous point, but the religious spirit will often take contradictory positions in its drive for self-preservation and exaltation. This use of emotionalism would include such things as requiring weeping and wailing as evidence of repentance, or "falling under the power" as evidence that one has been touched by God. Both of these can be evidences of the true work of the Holy Spirit; it is when we require these manifestations that we are beginning to move in another spirit.

During the First Great Awakening, Jonathan Edwards' meetings would often have some of the toughest, most rebellious men falling to the ground and staying there for up to twenty-four hours. They got up changed, and such strange manifestations of the Holy Spirit fueled the Great Awakenings. Even so, Edwards stated that people faking the manifestations did more to bring an end to the Great Awakening than the enemies of the revival!

16. Will be encouraged when their ministries look better than others. We could include in this being discouraged when it seems that others are looking better or growing faster than we are.

17. Will glory more in what God did in the past than in what He is doing in the present. God has not changed; He is the same yesterday, today, and forever. The veil has been removed, and we can be as close to God today as anyone ever has been in the past. A religious spirit will always seek to focus our attention on works and on making comparisons, rather than on simply drawing closer to the Lord.

18. Will tend to be suspicious of, or to oppose, new movements, churches, etc. This is an obvious symptom of jealousy, a primary fruit of the religious spirit, or the pride that asserts that God would not do anything new without doing it through them. Of course, those with such a mentality are seldom used by the Lord to birth new works.

19. Will tend to reject spiritual manifestations that they do not understand. This is a symptom of the

pride and arrogance of presuming that our opinions are the same as God's. True humility keeps us teachable and open, patiently waiting for fruit before making judgments. True discernment enables us to look for and hope for the best, not the worst. For this reason, we are exhorted to "**...examine everything carefully; hold fast to that which is good** [not what is bad]" (**I Thessalonians 5:21**).

20. Will overreact to carnality in the church. The truth is there is probably far more carnality in the church and a lot less of the Holy Spirit than even the most critical person has guessed. It is important that we learn to discern between them in order to be delivered from our carnality and grow in our submission to the Holy Spirit. But the critical person will annihilate those who may still be 60 percent carnal, but were 95 percent carnal last year. Instead, we need to recognize that people are making progress, and do what we can to help them along the way.

21. Will overreact to immaturity in the church. There is an immaturity that is acceptable to the Lord. A two-year old is immature when compared to a nine-year old, but that is to be expected. In fact, he may be very mature for a two-year old. The idealistic religious spirit only sees the immaturity, without considering the other important factors.

22. Will be overly prone to view supernatural manifestations as evidence of God's approval. This is just another form of keeping score and comparing ourselves with others. Some of Jesus' greatest miracles,

such as walking on water, were seen by only a few. He was doing His works to glorify the Father, not Himself. Those who use the evidence of miracles to promote and build their own ministries and reputations have made a serious departure from the path of life.

23. Will be unable to join anything that they do not deem perfect or nearly perfect. The Lord joined, and even gave His life for, the fallen human race. Such is the nature of those who abide in Him.

24. Will be overly paranoid of the religious spirit. We do not get free of something by fearing it, but by overcoming it with faith in Christ Jesus.

25. Will have the tendency to glory in anything but the cross of Jesus, what He has accomplished, and who He is. If we are building our lives, ministries, or churches on anything but these, we are building on a shaky foundation that will not stand.

Scoring on the Test

We are probably all subject to the religious spirit to at least some degree. Paul exhorted: **"Test yourselves to see if you are in the faith..." (II Corinthians 13:5).** First, he did not say to "test your neighbor" or to "test your pastor," but to **"test yourselves."** Using this test to measure others can be a symptom that we have a serious problem. If this chapter has given you illumination about problems in another person or ministry, be sure that you respond in the Holy Spirit, heeding Paul's warning to the Galatians:

Brethren, even if a man is caught in any trespass, you who are spiritual restore such a one in a spirit of gentleness; each one looking to yourself, lest you too be tempted (Galatians 6:1).

Special Acknowledgment

Some of the materials used in this part of the book, as well as a few of the warning signs at the end, were derived from Jack Deere's outstanding tape series *Exposing the Religious Spirit*, which is available through MorningStar Publications.

Part IV

THE GATES OF HELL
AND THE
DOORS OF HEAVEN

Chapter Ten

Understanding Spiritual Gates

The gates of hell are the entrances through which evil gains access to this world. Likewise, the doors of heaven are the openings through which divine grace and truth flow to the world. We are now entering the period when the gates of hell and the doors of heaven will be fully opened. It is imperative that we are able to recognize each, and use the authority given to us to close the gates of hell while opening the doors of heaven.

Spiritual Boundaries

These spiritual "gates" and "doors" are often cities, where people are concentrated in greater numbers. The conflict between the kingdom of God and this present evil age is not over territory, but over people. When the Lord moves to impact a nation, He is not after their land, but after their hearts. He sees nations more in the light of cultures, customs, and behavior, rather than borders. In fact, spiritual borders are often different from natural borders—the spiritual influence of a city may reach far beyond its designated boundaries. We must learn to distinguish spiritual borders by the boundaries of their influence.

A striking example of this is Cologne, Germany, which has been one of the most influential cities in world history, even though that influence has remained remarkably hidden and obscure. Some of the most deadly theologies and philosophies the world has ever known originated in Cologne. It is possible that more bloodshed has resulted from the influence of this city than of any empire or superpower in world history. Neither have any of these diabolical theologies or philosophies that originated from Cologne yet been overcome. They continue to sprout and cause rivers of death to flow in almost every new generation. We will begin to address some of these doctrines of demons in this chapter by exposing their source. However, this is only the first step in a long and difficult march to defeat and close these gates.

Just winning battles against this darkness is not enough. Like Joshua at Ai, we must learn to hold out our spear until the enemy is utterly destroyed (see Joshua 8:18). If we do not complete the job, our children will be confronted by the same deadly enemy.

A Spiritual History of the Crusades

The Province of Cologne was founded at the very time of the birth of Christ. Emperor Augustus' niece,

Agrippina senior, who was said to be a descendant of Aphrodite, the goddess of love, married Germanicus, the conqueror of Gaul, in Cologne in 15 A.D. In 16 A.D., she gave birth to a daughter, Agrippina Jr., in the Oppidum-Obiorum in Cologne, a Roman and Germanic cult center which was situated where the Cathedral of Cologne now stands. Agrippina Jr. became the mother of the Roman Emperor Nero, one of the most cruel and demented of the Roman emperors. It was under Nero that the Christians were first fed to the lions in the Circus Maximus. It was also Nero who condemned both Peter and Paul to execution in Rome.

Thus it was that the first great Roman persecution against the church had its roots in Cologne. Owing to the fact that Nero's mother, and the subsequent emperor, Caligula, both came from Cologne, from 69 A.D. the city became the capital of the Western Roman Empire, which it remained for two centuries. Provinces governed from Cologne included France, Spain, Germany, and Britain. During that time, Cologne gained considerable influence and became the host of every conceivable god and temple.

The Sin of Achan

In the year 313, Emperor Constantine, who made Christianity the state religion of Rome, sent a bishop called Maternus to Cologne, Trier, and Tongern to destroy their idols and temples. However, not all of these idols were destroyed. Some were actually used as building materials for the first Christian churches.

This could be compared to the sin of Achan, who tried to preserve some of the treasure of Jericho in spite of the decree to destroy it all (see Joshua 7). Just as Achan's sin resulted in the subsequent defeat of Israel before the city of Ai, preserving some of the pagan idols of Cologne seemingly resulted in a tragic parallel. Though the structures were meant to be Christian, some of the most anti-Christian evils the world would ever experience would arise from their region.

Many in the church believe that they can mix human and even cultic philosophies, such as Masonry, into the fabric of the church or their own spiritual lives without consequence. This is a terrible delusion. The Lord will not share His temple with idols. Judgment may not always come immediately as it did at Ai; sometimes the Lord will even wait for a generation or two before bringing judgment, as He did with some of the kings of Israel. But such presumption will always result in defeat, captivity, or destruction.

The roots of many destructive heresies in the church today began long ago in the heart of just one person who compromised like Achan. As we move to possess our promised land, we will learn quickly that every "Achan" must be removed from the camp, or else the whole camp will be defeated. This is why Paul, in his first letter to the Corinthians, had the church remove the sinner from their midst (see I Corinthians 5).

Every time those in spiritual leadership fail to take the proper action against sin in the camp, they allow the seeds to be sown for future defeat, division and destruction. However, we are in the age of grace. This does not mean that we tolerate the sin, but that we are willing to accept the repentant sinner back into our camp, just as Paul exhorted the Corinthians to do in his second letter (see II Corinthians 2:18).

The Seed of the Crusades

In 632, the Muslims began making advances into Europe and the Middle East. In 638, Khalif Omar conquered Jerusalem, which had been held by the Christian Byzantine Empire (which later developed into the Orthodox Church). The Empire's capital was Constantinople, now the modern city of Istanbul. It was believed that this empire would never fall because it was Christian. Nevertheless, the Turks, led by Alp Arslam, destroyed the Byzantine army in Mantzikert on Friday, August 19, 1071, and took captive the Christian Emperor of Byzantine, Romanos Diogenes.

The Muslims then advanced deeper into European territory, targeting France, Spain, and the Balkans. As their progress began to threaten all of Europe, a letter from the Christian bishop of Jerusalem convinced the Pope to devise a strategy for retaking the ancient city. This would also relieve the pressure on Europe, requiring the Muslims to return to defend their own lands.

So the Pope convinced sovereigns and knights of the necessity of his plan to retake Jerusalem. Peasants, the homeless, and even prostitutes, wanting to be free from the bondage of serfdom, were also recruited. The

Pope then claimed to possess a letter from heaven which appointed him to summon the European nations to liberate the Holy Sepulcher.

In March 1096, Peter of Amiens (also called "Peter the Hermit") left on his donkey, arriving in Trier just before Easter. On Easter Sunday he marched into Cologne with about ten thousand men. He then sent out preachers to proclaim the "gospel" of the Crusades and to raise further support in the Rhineland area. Consequently, his army grew to a total of thirty thousand men.

Peter was thus given the credit for starting the Crusades that would change the known world, leaving some of the deepest cultural wounds between Christians and Muslims, wounds which remain to this day. He also began a persecution against the Jews, with doctrines that would ultimately lead to some of the most diabolical atrocities in history.

The Seed of the Holocaust

Needing more money for their venture, the Crusaders determined to force the Jews to support the mission, as they were the primary bankers of that time. Many of the knights financed their participation in the Crusades by mortgaging their estates to the banks. Then the Crusaders decided that they did not want to pay the banks back, so they declared that it was a divine mandate to turn against the Jews because "they killed Jesus on the cross."

Gottfried of Bouillon was the sovereign of Lower-Lothringen, which also included the Ardennes, present-day Holland, and the Rhine Provinces of Cologne. He issued a decree that all the remaining Jews living in Lower-Lothringen should be killed in order to atone for Christ's death. As a result, the Jews in Cologne and Mainz gave Gottfried five hundred silver coins in order to buy their protection, which was used to pay for and arm his forces. This method of raising financial support quickly became popular throughout Europe. In this way, the Jews found themselves not only loaning money to the Crusaders through their banks, but paying ransom money to bishops and knights as well.

Even after the Jews had paid for protection, Rhineland Count Emmerich began killing the Jews in the region of Cologne. Peter's army then attacked the Jews in Prague while Gottschalk, Peter's former pupil, massacred them in Regensburg. Thus began almost nine hundred years during which the Jewish people would be subject to continuous threats of annihilation. In one of the greatest perversions of the Savior's message, the people through whom the Prince of Peace came were threatened with extinction by the very ones who claimed to be His ambassadors.

During the following centuries, Jews were periodically assaulted and robbed, and at times whole ghettos were massacred, sparing only those who would submit themselves to baptism. There were many Christians who took stands against this tragic intolerance, such as Bernard of Claireveaux, who tried earnestly to protect Jews from the bigotry and fanatical violence of the church, but with little success.

These attacks on the Jews were not limited to the Roman church. With the emergence of the Protestant church in the 1500s, theologies were also promulgated within that branch of Christendom which continued this persecution, and ultimately led to some of the worst atrocities of all in Nazi Germany. The remarkable Jews have survived each successive and seemingly more vicious assault—but the wounds these people have received from Christians over the centuries have grown very deep. This has caused them to equate Christianity more with their destruction than with their salvation.

Many Jews have tried magnanimously to keep alive the memory that with each attack there were always some Christians of a different spirit who came to their aid. Understandably, this has created a powerful ambivalence in the Jewish community toward the church. The wounds can only be healed by an extraordinary outpouring of love and grace, which is precisely what the church must demonstrate in these last days.

The Crusades and Cologne

At the end of April 1096, Peter of Amiens and his army marched from Cologne. They arrived in Constantinople on August 1. Since an army of that size (which was also escorted by women and children) had to be fed and provided for, and because there was very little discipline, they left a wide trail of pillage and destruction. Soon they became odious even to the Christian cities they were supposedly marching to protect.

Most in this first crusade had little or no military experience, and so it was recommended that they wait in Constantinople for the better trained army of knights that was being prepared in Europe. However, because of the rising strife between the Crusaders and the local population, it was decided that the army should march from Constantinople as quickly as possible.

They left on October 21, and were quickly defeated by the Turks at Civitot. The entire army of thirty thousand, including the women and children, were killed. Only Peter and a few knights survived the massacre and escaped back to Constantinople.

Gottfried of Bouillon departed from Lower-Lothringen in 1096 at about the same time that Peter of Amiens was arriving in Constantinople. After marching for weeks along the Rhine and the Danube, he finally reached Constantinople at Christmas. By the most conservative estimates, his army numbered no less than six hundred thousand.

Peter, who had survived the battle against the Turks, joined Gottfried and took the lead of the new "Farmer's Army." At the end of April 1097, the Crusaders set off from Pelecanum near Constantinople. They crossed the Bosporus in October and besieged Antioch, which fell eight months later on June 3.

Defeat in Victory

On January 13, 1099, the army started for Jerusalem, and came to the city on June 7. At midday on Friday, July 15, the Holy City fell. It is a biblical truth that many of God's victories look like defeats to the natural man, the cross being the greatest example of this. When Jerusalem was captured by the Christians, the converse of this principle was also shown: What may have appeared in the natural to be a great victory for the church would live in infamy as one of her greatest defeats.

The Muslim mayor had been relatively tolerant with all of his citizens, including the Christians and Jews. He allowed them their own places of worship, and freedom to come and go as they pleased. He even allowed the Christians in Jerusalem to go over to the side of the Crusaders during the siege. When it was obvious that the Christians would prevail, the mayor and his subjects likewise expected a high degree of chivalry from their conquerors. They were terribly mistaken.

Many had gathered under a Christian banner, where they had been promised amnesty. The Crusaders, thus having them surrounded, slaughtered them all. The Jews of the city fled into the synagogue. Having them trapped inside, the Crusaders torched the building, killing all of its inhabitants in a gruesome spectacle.

This was a deliberate strategy to eradicate all non-Christians so that Jerusalem could become a Christian city. The triumphant Crusaders, many completely covered in the blood of their victims, gathered at the Holy Sepulcher, and weeping with joy, offered thanksgiving for their great "victory." More than fifty thousand Saracens alone were killed in this terrible massacre.

Gottfried of Bouillon, the first Christian sovereign and primary instigator of the massacre, died one year later on July 18, 1100, and King Balduin I became his successor. The Kingdom of Jerusalem existed for eighty-seven years until the Empire was conquered by the Muslim king, Saladin. Crusaders repeatedly marched for the next two hundred years, but they never managed to retake Jerusalem.

Many of the leaders of the church during this time were appalled at the atrocities of the Crusaders. Some even demanded that those responsible should be excommunicated. There were also many noble and courageous souls who participated in the Crusades. Some were obviously motivated by a sincere desire to recover the honor of the name of the Lord in Jerusalem. Even so, regardless of how noble our motives may be, whenever we use methods that are contrary to the fruit of the Holy Spirit, evil will be the result.

From their beginning to their end, the Crusades released some of the most evil forces, philosophies, and theologies into the world. Their fruit has been that countless millions have been separated from the gospel by the huge barriers which these events erected between peoples. The evil strongholds empowered by these misguided tragedies must be addressed in order for the gospel to be freely released in some of the most strategic regions of the world.

The Spiritual History of Communism

On July 23, 1164, Archbishop Reinald of Dassel brought what were supposedly the bones of the three wise men to Cologne. Emperor Friedrichs Barbarossa had given them to the city as a reward for the archbishop's loyalty. In 1181, the golden coffin made to contain them was completed (which can still be seen in Cologne today). Consequently, many pilgrims from all over the Western world came to the city to venerate the golden shrine and the bones. As the crowds of pilgrims became more numerous, a larger cathedral became necessary. On August 15, 1248, the foundation of the Cologne cathedral was laid as a place of honor for the bones of the three wise men.

The building of this great cathedral continued for more than three hundred years until it was abruptly stopped. In a remarkable legend recorded in the city's history, it is said that the master builder had to make a pact with the devil to complete the project. The pact stated that an aqueduct had to be built from the city of Trier to Cologne before the devil would allow the cathedral to be finished. This was so that water could flow from Satan's throne just as it did from the throne of God. This would be a river of death that would ultimately eclipse all of the previous rivers of death that had originated from Cologne, resulting in an estimated one hundred million killed in the twentieth century alone.

This is an official German banknote that was circulated in 1922. In the top view, we see the back of the note depicting the chief engineer making a covenant with the devil to finish the cathedral. The inscription above it reads, "Emergency money of the city of Cologne," and underneath, "The dome (cathedral) master builder and the devil." The writing on the front of the note is translated, "City of Cologne 1922. Voucher in the value of fifty pennies."

Amazingly, the work on the cathedral was stopped from 1560 until 1842. In 1818 Karl Marx, the founder of socialism and the world's most powerful atheistic system, was born in Trier. In 1842 he moved from Trier to Cologne, and work on the cathedral began again. It was finally completed in 1880. This was no coincidence—the pact with the devil had been honored.

From 1842 until 1843, Karl Marx was the chief editor of the *Rheinische Zeitung* newspaper published in Cologne. In 1848 he became its publisher. It was from this position that he printed *The Communist Manifesto*. On May 6, 1849, his communist broadsheets were thrown into the crowd assembled in the Gurzenich Hall in Cologne. This marked the birth of the Communist movement, led by Karl Marx and Friedrich Engels. Other powerful leaders of this new movement begun in Cologne included: Ferdinand Lassaile, Andreas Gottschalk, and Matthilde Franziska Anneke.

Shutting the Gates of Hell

As the birthplace of the mother of the first Roman persecutor of the church, the Crusades, the Christian persecution of the Jews, and then communism, Cologne has been the womb of the greatest human tragedies in history. However, the way that the Lord shuts the gates of hell is to open a door in heaven. Light is more powerful than darkness. When you open your shades at night, darkness does not come in; light shines out into the dark.

God's strategy for Cologne is to open a window from heaven there, to make it a testimony of His power of redemption. The Lord will raise up new armies of Crusaders from Cologne and Germany, with weapons that are not carnal but spiritual. They will bring life and healing to all of the places where the Crusaders of old once brought death and destruction. The Lord always overcomes evil with good.

It is interesting that Robert Blum and Moses Hess also started their careers in Cologne, just as the construction of the Cathedral was being completed. They are considered by many to be the modern founders of Zionism. Just as the enemy has been so successful in sowing tares in the Lord's wheat fields, the Lord often sows wheat in the enemy's fields of tares. The city where the most deadly persecution of the Jews originated is also regarded as a birthplace of the movement that resulted in the establishment of the modern state of Israel.

Moses Hess actually followed Karl Marx as an editor of the *Rheinische Zeitung* newspaper in Cologne, where he published a pamphlet called *Rome and Jerusalem—the Final Question of Nationality*, in the 1860s. In 1891, Dr. Bodenheimer of Cologne, who was one of the three major founders of Zionism, wrote his poem, *Vision*, which prophetically described the future establishment of Israel.

Hess began to correspond with Dr. Theodore Herzl in 1896, the year that Herzl wrote his landmark book,

The Jewish State. Cologne then became the home of the global Zionist movement and the Jewish National Foundation, which began to purchase property in Palestine. When Herzl died in 1904, David Wolffsohn of Cologne succeeded him as the head of the Zionist movement, keeping its headquarters in Cologne.

It is also interesting to note that after Wolffsohn died and Bodenheimer retired, Weizmann took over the organization and moved its headquarters to London. This also followed the work of Karl Marx, who, having been expelled by the Prussian government, had moved his headquarters to London.

Nearly five centuries earlier, William Tyndale, the famous English reformer, was expelled from London and went to Cologne. It was Tyndale who first translated the Scriptures into the common language, and is called "The morning star of the Reformation." He actually had his first Bibles printed in Cologne.

Special Acknowledgment

Special thanks to Norbert Siegrist of Christliche Gemeinde Koln for sharing his extraordinary research on the city of Cologne for this chapter.

Chapter Eleven

When Heaven and Hell Collide

When the enemy comes in like a flood, the Lord will raise up a standard against him (see Isaiah 59:19 KJV). The Lord is raising up, through His church, a people who live by the opposite spirit of what has been manifested through the strongholds of Satan. In the place that seems to have been the very seat of Satan for the past few centuries, where some of the most terrible sins have abounded, grace will abound even more.

Job is one of the great biblical examples of how the Lord uses His people as a witness to principalities and powers. The Lord actually asked Satan if he had considered Job (see Job 1:8), purposely drawing the enemy's attention to him. He then gave the enemy permission to assault him, with the only stipulation being that he could not take Job's life. Satan has likewise been given almost free reign to assault the church, but he cannot destroy it, and ultimately it will come back twice as great as it was at the beginning.

Moses restrained the Lord from destroying Israel because he knew that the whole world would say that God could deliver His people from Egypt, but He did not have the power to bring them into the Promised Land. Satan's accusation against God in regard to the church is that He can redeem us, but He cannot really change us.

Just as Job stood the test, the Lord will have a church that testifies to all of creation, throughout all eternity, that God not only has the power to redeem us, but also to change us and bring us all the way into the Promised Land. Like Job, we may be a mess for a while, but there will be a church that remains faithful through all of her trials. Then, after the church learns to pray even for her accusers and tormentors, she will be given a double portion of what she had before (see Job 42:10-12).

Why Look Back?

Many believe that it is wrong to uncover the terrible mistakes made by the church historically, such as the Crusades. However, it is quite clear that the greatest mistake of all has come from trying to forget them. Just as the world shudders at the thought of Germany forgetting her tragic history under the Nazis, knowing that she could then repeat it, the world also shudders at this same terrible folly of the church. There are good reasons why the world is appalled by the thought of the church again asserting political power—our historic use of it has ended in horrible abuses and tragedies.

This does not mean that the church cannot use political power for good, but until we recognize and understand our mistakes, we are doomed to repeat them. The history of the church has basically been the continued repetition of the same mistakes. Powerful forces are still working in the church to lay the same stumbling blocks before this generation that caused our forefathers to stumble. However, the Lord is preparing to give us the wisdom to use these same stumbling blocks as material for sealing some of the most powerful gates of hell.

We Have Committed the Same Sins

The Crusades are only one example in the history of the church of tragically misguided religious zeal. No Muslim despot or Ayatollah in history has been as ruthless and cruel as some leaders of the church during the Inquisitions. We may protest that they were the works of the Roman Catholics, but the Protestants were guilty of all of the same errors, if only to a lesser degree because they had less political power.

As Evangelicals, we may point at the Catholics and Protestants and declare that we are different, but we, too, are guilty of the same sins. We can protest that the Catholics have a pope who has usurped Christ's rightful place as the Head of the church, but we have many leaders or "popes" who do the same. We abhor the veneration of Mary the mother of Jesus, but we worship our churches. We are shocked by prayers being made to saints, but we are constantly raising up our own leaders as idols to mediate for us.

We can become indignant as we read about the Catholic practice of selling indulgences (decrees sold that supposedly released the holders, or deceased relatives, from the consequences of their sins); and we should be, as this is one of the greatest affronts to the cross, by which the grace of God was purchased for man. Even so, for almost a decade one could hardly turn on an evangelical television or radio program without hearing promises of blessings if we would just give to their ministry, which is the same diabolical attempt to sell the grace of God.

We are appalled as we study the Crusades, which were claimed to be expeditions for the glory of God and the name of Christ. Indeed, they manifested some of the darkest evils of fallen human nature, resulting in far more damnation than salvation. However, almost every "crusade" the church has initiated since has resulted in far more being turned away from the Lord than are turned to Him. The Crusaders claimed to carry their swords for the sake of the cross, the very symbol of salvation, yet they ruthlessly hacked men, women, and children to death. We have been given an even greater sword, the Word of God, yet we, too, often use it to wound and destroy the ones that we claim to want to save and heal.

The Death Cycle Must Be Broken

The maxim has proven true that "Those who do not know history are doomed to repeat it." The history of the church is one of the greatest proofs of this. The cycle of previous spiritual generations waging war against subsequent movements continues unabated because of theologies that were released into the church centuries ago through the gates of hell. It is now time for those gates to be shut. To do this, we must understand them, and must repent of the sins that they unleashed. We may protest that we have not yet committed such sins, but we will if we do not address them properly.

It is no accident that the great restoration ministries in Scripture, such as Ezra and Nehemiah, gave so much attention to repenting for "the sins of our fathers." They understood the biblical principle that the sins of the fathers are visited upon the children, generation after generation (see Exodus 20:5). This is not for the purpose of punishing the children for what their fathers have done, but rather it is recognition that every time there is a sin, there is a wound. Contrary to popular belief, wounds do not heal themselves with time; as time goes on, they become infected unless they are properly dressed and closed. The way that they are dressed and closed is through repentance, which releases the power of the cross.

The Scriptures declare that there are sins which will defile the land in addition to defiling those who commit them. Procedures were given in the Law of Moses for cleansing the land from such sins. This is why we see in II Samuel 21 that a famine came on the land during the reign of David. When he inquired of the Lord as to why the famine had come, the Lord answered, **"It is for Saul and his bloody house, because he put the Gibeonites to death" (II Samuel 21:1).**

To remove the curse, David had to go to the Gibeonites and make restitution for the sins of Saul. Even though David had nothing to do with these sins, he had to make restitution for the land. The restitution was to give the Gibeonites Saul's remaining sons so that they could hang them on trees. This happened because under the Law, restitution was "an eye for an eye, a tooth for a tooth" (see Exodus 21:24).

We are no longer under the Law, but under grace. The cross has made restitution for all of the sins of this world, including all of the tragic sins that the church has committed. However, sins still defile much of the land, and curses remain that release and give authority to evil principalities and powers. Why? Because the cross has not yet been applied to them. Jesus paid the price for the sins of the whole world, but the whole world has not been saved, because it has not yet embraced the cross.

The Ministry of Reconciliation

It is our commission as priests, and as ministers of reconciliation, to carry the power of the cross to this world. Because we are now in the age of grace, the procedures of the Law will no longer cleanse the land—God's grace must be applied. We do not appeal to the Law, but to the cross. Even so, if there is to be reconciliation, the cross must be applied to every wound caused by sin, including these deep, historic, cultural wounds. Then the power of the gospel will be released.

How is the cross applied? Through the humility of repentance. Grace has been popularly defined as "undeserved favor." That is not the complete definition, but it is accurate enough for our present focus. As soon as we begin to feel that we deserve the favor of God, we have made a departure from the path of life.

So how do we attain God's grace? **"God is opposed to the proud, but gives grace to the humble" (James 4:6).** Simple humility can release the grace of God to us, and to our land. It is a terrible pride for us to say that we are different from our forefathers. It takes the grace of humility to acknowledge that we have all sinned and come short of His grace (see Romans 3:23). That simple humility can release the grace.

True Humility

The most basic quality of true humility is the knowledge of our dependency on God. Only true humility will keep us in the grace of God, which will give us the light to see all of the stumbling blocks, traps, and diversions that continually try to assault us. Humility can also open our eyes to **"the iniquities** of our fathers" (see **Daniel 9:16**) of which we must repent in order to bring restoration.

David was not allowed to build a permanent house for the Lord because he was a man who had shed blood. The permanent house that Solomon constructed was to be a representation of the permanent kingdom that would be established by Jesus, who did not come to shed the blood of others, but to give His own blood for our salvation. When Solomon's temple was dedicated, the Lord gave a promise that transcended the age of the Law and pointed to the kingdom of our Lord Jesus:

> **If I shut up the heavens so that there is no rain, or if I command the locust to devour the land, or if I send pestilence among My people,**
>
> **and My people who are called by My name humble themselves and pray, and seek My face and turn from their wicked ways, then I will hear from heaven, will forgive their sin, and will heal their land (II Chronicles 7:13-14).**

No longer would the healing of the land require the restitution required by the Law, but the Lord's people could humble themselves, pray, seek the Lord, and turn from their own wicked ways, and the Lord would hear, forgive the sin, and heal the land.

We can try to beat up principalities in order to bring revival, but sometimes there are curses on the land that give them the authority to be there, and there will be no revival until the Lord's people repent of these sins. When there is a curse on the land, the church has the authority, through humility and repentance, to bring healing to the land. This is why the whole creation is groaning, waiting for the manifestation of the sons of God (see Romans 8:19-22).

We Are Guilty

When we study church history, it is easy to judge and criticize all of our church fathers, whether they were Catholics, Protestants, Evangelicals, or otherwise. We can even find cause to criticize recent spiritual movements. However, this criticism only ensures that we, too, will fall short. There is a difference between criticism and the righteous judgment that we must use in order to remove sin from the camp.

Even the most terrible evil resident in the **"man of sin" (see II Thessalonians 2:3 NKJV)** is actually the sin of man that is in all of us. We all desire to be "worshiped" and to have influence, authority, and the chief seat of honor. If we no longer have these evil motives, it is only because the grace of God has delivered us. If we begin to think that we no longer have these evil desires because we ourselves are good, we have at that point departed from grace, and they will come back like a flood.

One of the most tragic mistakes that we can make is to look at the sins of our forefathers and think that we are better than they were. We must not consider the sins of the historic church, or the contemporary church, as their problems, but as our problems. If we are ever going to receive deliverance from the sins that are passed from generation to generation, it will come when we humble ourselves, identifying with the tragic evils that we, the church, have committed. We must repent and seek the Lord for grace and forgiveness from these tragic, historic sins of the church.

The whole world was wounded and cursed by the fall of Adam, who is the forefather of us all. The Lord Jesus, even though He was completely innocent, identified with the whole sin of man, taking it upon Himself so that He could make restitution. How much more should we be able to identify with the sins of the world, humbling ourselves and repenting for the sins of mankind, interceding to release the forgiveness that Jesus purchased for the whole world? What we release in the heavens in this way will be released upon the earth.

It is in this spirit—not condemning, but rather seeking to bring restoration and reconciliation—that we will continue to examine some of the gates through which hell has gained access or influence into the church. As the Lord Jesus warned:

> **"Enter by the narrow gate; for the gate is wide, and the way is broad that leads to destruction, and many are those who enter by it.**

> **"For the gate is small, and the way is narrow that leads to life, and few are those who find it.**

"Beware of the false prophets, who come to you in sheep's clothing, but inwardly are ravenous wolves.

"You will know them by their fruits. Grapes are not gathered from thorn bushes, nor figs from thistles, are they?

"Even so, every good tree bears good fruit; but the rotten tree bears bad fruit.

"A good tree cannot produce bad fruit, nor can a bad tree produce good fruit.

"Every tree that does not bear good fruit is cut down and thrown into the fire.

"So then, you will know them by their fruits" (Matthew 7:13-20).

Can good and evil come out of the same tree? Yes! Just as they may both come from the Tree of the Knowledge of Good and Evil. However, good fruit and bad fruit cannot come from the same tree. A foundation for some of the greatest errors the church has ever fallen into is the failure to understand that the "good" from the Tree of Knowledge is just as deadly as the "evil" that comes from the same tree. The knowledge of good and evil has the same root, and its fruit will result in death regardless of whether it comes in a "good" form or an "evil" form. Human "goodness" is as deadly a poison as any human evil.

Once we understand that the good from the Tree of Knowledge is just as deadly as the evil, we also begin to recognize that it is far more deceptive, and therefore has been far more successful in spreading death. One of the ultimate issues facing every Christian is how to discern between what is good and what is God. Only that which originates with God will give life.

Because this difference between the Tree of the Knowledge of Good and Evil and the Tree of Life is covered in depth in my book, *There Were Two Trees in the Garden*, I will not belabor this point anymore here. However, we must understand this as the reason behind the Lord's continued discourse:

"Not everyone who says to Me, 'Lord, Lord,' will enter the kingdom of heaven; but he who does the will of My Father who is in heaven.

"Many will say to Me on that day, 'Lord, Lord, did we not prophesy in Your name, and in Your name cast out demons, and in Your name perform many miracles?'

"And then I will declare to them, 'I never knew you; depart from Me, you who practice lawlessness'" (Matthew 7:21-23).

This warning highlights several startling facts. First, we can call Jesus "Lord" continually, but still not enter His kingdom. Second, we can do many great works using His name and still not enter, because we are in fact practicing lawlessness.

This corroborates the Lord's warning in Matthew 24:5: **"For many will come in My name, saying, 'I**

am the Christ,' and will mislead many." This text has often been quoted as meaning that many would come claiming to be the Christ, and would mislead many. But that is not actually what it says. Jesus is literally saying that many will come in "His name," saying that He (Jesus) is the Christ, and yet will be deceivers who mislead many. History has adequately verified this, as many "Christian leaders" have arisen, claiming to come in the name of Jesus and declaring Him to be the Christ, and yet have misled multitudes.

How could the church, which God planted, have brought forth such evil and such good fruit throughout history? First, the church in this world is not just a single plant. The Apostle Paul called the church **"God's field" (see I Corinthians 3:9).** In this field many theologies have been planted—some for good and some for evil, some for life and some that have brought forth death. The Lord Himself warned that every time He planted wheat in a field, the enemy would come along and plant tares in the same field (see Matthew 13:24-30).

One of our tragic mistakes is that we have failed to judge the fruit of many of the theologies and doctrines that have been sown in the church. It is right that we challenge them with the Scriptures, but some doctrines which initially appear to be biblical, can still bring forth evil fruit. The enemy himself used Scripture in this way to tempt Jesus, and the enemy himself will often come to us with Scripture to tempt us. That is why the Lord never said that we would know His people by how biblical they were, but by their fruit (see Matthew 12:33).

The Evil Root

There has been one doctrine that has proven to be the most devastating throughout history, and was a main source of all of the terrible follies discussed in this section. It is still one of the most popular teachings in the church today. This is basically the delusion that we can accomplish the purposes of God by might and power. However, as the prophet solemnly warned, it is "**'Not by might, nor by power, but by My Spirit,' says the Lord of hosts**" (Zechariah 4:6).

The Lord is called by many titles in Scripture, and each one is used strategically. It is no accident that He calls Himself the **"Lord of hosts"** or the "Lord of armies" in this text. His army does not use military might or political power, but that which is infinitely more powerful—the Spirit of Truth. The truth, spoken under the anointing, is more powerful than all the weapons and bombs this world can muster. Why is it that we, who have been entrusted with the most powerful weapons of all, continually stoop to using those which are so inferior? As the apostle warned:

For though we walk in the flesh, we do not war according to the flesh,

for the weapons of our warfare are not of the flesh, but divinely powerful for the destruction of fortresses,

we are destroying speculations and every lofty thing raised up against the knowledge of God, and we are taking every thought captive to the obedience of Christ,

and we are ready to punish all dis-obedience, whenever your obedience is complete (II Corinthians 10:3-6).

When our obedience is complete—that is, when we are completely yielded to the Spirit, learning not to war in the flesh but only according to His divinely powerful weapons, we will be ready to "**punish all disobedience.**"

However, the church is not just called to "do something;" we are called to follow the Lamb where He is going. One of the reasons the Laodicean spirit prevails in much of the church is simply because many believers are worn-out from all the causes and projects that have not borne true spiritual fruit. Activism that is not in submission to Him will ultimately result in an even greater retreat by those who are injured by the extremes, and there will be injury.

We need zeal, but for the Lord and His purposes. Anything less is merely "zealotry," which is just another form of humanism, even fanaticism, regardless of how righteous the goals are. It is not just sacrifice, but obedience, that counts.

Chapter Twelve

The Two Mandates

The Lord has given two different mandates to two entirely different forms of government—the civil government and the church. He has given a mandate to civil governments to keep order on this earth. They keep this order with "carnal weapons"—the sword. That is why Paul wrote:

> Let every person be in subjection to the governing authorities. For there is no authority except from God, and those which exist are established by God.

> Therefore, he who resists authority has opposed the ordinance of God; and they who have opposed will receive condemnation upon themselves.

> For rulers are not a cause of fear for good behavior, but for evil. Do you want to have

no fear of authority? Do what is good, and you will have praise from the same;

for it is a minister of God to you for good. But if you do what is evil, be afraid; for it does not bear the sword for nothing; for it is a minister of God, an avenger who brings wrath upon the one who practices evil.

Wherefore it is necessary to be in subjection, not only because of wrath, but also for conscience' sake.

For because of this you also pay taxes, for rulers are servants of God... (Romans 13:1-6).

This exhortation was written during the reign of Nero, the same Roman Emperor we discussed earlier. He was one of the most wicked men to ever hold a scepter, and he initiated one of the bloodiest persecutions ever raised against the church. Nero eventually took Paul's own life! This passage in Romans 13 was written after the apostle had already spent many years being persecuted at the hands of civil governments.

All authority in both heaven and earth has been given to Christ, but He has not yet directly taken His authority over the earth, nor has He given it to us. He has not directly taken His authority because He has not yet manifestly set up His kingdom on the earth. However, He has indirectly taken His authority over the earth, because there is no earthly ruler or spiritual principality that gains dominion without His approval—even the most wicked.

A Higher Power

The church has also been given authority from God. The power entrusted to the church is much greater than that entrusted to civil authorities. Civil authority is temporary—ours is eternal. They can change laws, but we can change men.

Margaret Thatcher, the former Prime Minister of Great Britain, once observed, "The veneer of civilization is very thin." This remark was made after watching people behave like animals when the power went out in New York City. When the lights and alarms go off, and the police are not immediately present, the true nature of mankind is quickly revealed. This "thin veneer" is the realm of civil authority. We need the lights, the alarms, and the police, and we should thank God for the civil authorities that provide them, but their realm of authority is limited.

In contrast, true spiritual authority is as limitless as eternity. Spiritual authority is not found in the streetlights that keep people in check—it is the light in people's hearts that compels them to do right even when the lights go off and the police are not around. It is this light that keeps young men and women pure, or if they have made a mistake, shows them such love and respect for life that they would not even consider getting an abortion.

King David is one of the great biblical examples of one who walked in true spiritual authority. He is also one of the great types of Christ, who will one day exercise both spiritual and civil authority over the earth, along with His church. Even when David was unjustly persecuted by the civil authority of his nation, and even though he had already been anointed to take Saul's place, David would not lift his own hand **"against the Lord's anointed" (see I Samuel 26:11).** His heart even smote him for cutting off the edge of Saul's robe (see I Samuel 24).

It was this great respect for every authority established by God which enabled David to build a house and a throne that would last forever—for Jesus Himself is seated **"upon the throne of David" (see Isaiah 9:7 NKJV).** One who walks in true spiritual authority will never take a position by his own hand, but will patiently wait for the Spirit to make the way, even if it is a position in the realm of civil authority. If we aspire to sit with Jesus on His throne, it can only be accomplished this way.

The Lord is presently allowing His church, who is called to rule with Him, to be subject to all of the testings that David went through. The temptation of Jesus by Satan in the wilderness was basically an attempt to pressure Him to take His authority over the world prematurely, enabling Him to avoid the cross. This is also Satan's primary temptation for the church. He knows that if he can get us to seize temporal authority before we have been through the trials that are meant to prepare us for this rule, we will end up worshiping him by doing his bidding. Thus far he has been very successful with this temptation.

The Stumbling Block

There have been a number of Christians in history who were called to take a position in the realm of civil authority, and they accomplished great things for humanity. William Wilberforce, the Prime Minister of Great Britain who abolished slavery in the British Empire, is one. But even this great accomplishment was still just a superficial victory in the realm of the "thin veneer," as exploitation through colonization would continue for centuries, and economic oppression in many forms continues today. Even so, in the realm of human history this was a huge step in the right direction for mankind, and the great evangelists John Wesley and George Whitefield had much to do with it.

However, whenever the church has left her realm of authority to impose her will in the realm of civil authority, she has fallen to tragic and even diabolical excesses. The key here is that these mistakes have taken place whenever she has left her realm of authority. The church has been called to be the **"light of the world" (see Matthew 5:14)**—a force for good, upholding the standard of God's righteousness. But the trap that she has often fallen into has been to try to accomplish this from the realm of civil authority that was given to others.

The church will never become the light of the world by excelling at the ballot box. When the people came to make Jesus king, He fled to the mountains (see John 6:15). If the people make you king, who is going to actually rule? Although it seems very noble that the people wanted to make Jesus king, it was actually one of the most presumptuous acts in Scripture. The people thought that they could make God king! He was born King! The source of His authority never came from the people, but from the Father above. Likewise, the church's true authority comes from above, and every time she has sought authority from any other source the consequences have been devastating.

Our Sphere of Authority

Paul explained to the Corinthians that he had been given a sphere of authority that he would not presume to go beyond (see II Corinthians 10:13-14). Those who understand spiritual authority will be very conscious of the sphere that has been appointed to them, because to go beyond it invites disaster. Just as a policeman from Atlanta has no authority in Mexico City, and would probably get hurt if he tried to use it, we do not have spiritual authority beyond the realm that God has given to us. The sphere of authority given to the civil governments is different than that which is given to the church. Whenever the church has tried to accomplish its objectives by using the sphere appointed to the civil authorities, or whenever the civil authorities have tried to accomplish their ends by using the church, the result has been tragic.

The sphere of authority for civil governments is the realm of law, and the sphere of authority appointed to the church is the realm of the Spirit.

The boundaries of our sphere of authority can easily be recognized as the "fruit of the Spirit."

As Jesus said, **"If I cast out demons by the Spirit of God, then the kingdom of God has come upon you" (Matthew 12:28).** If we try to cast out these demons by any other spirit, we can be sure that the kingdom of darkness will come upon us, and we will be left wounded and naked, at best (see Acts 19:13-16).

The Lord Jesus never once tried to use the civil authorities to accomplish the Father's purposes; neither did the apostles or other leaders of the early church. They understood that to do so would have been to come down from the high position that they were given. They let Caesar have that which was his, and gave themselves to the things that were God's (see Matthew 22:15-21).

Prophetic Authority

The church is called to speak prophetically to governments, and it is that prophetic anointing which is a foundation of our mandated influence with governments. Prophetic authority is the moral authority and power of the truth, clearly articulated and established by a righteous life.

We cannot continue to expect the government to do our job. Not only abortion, but infanticide, were major problems in the first century Roman Empire, but the writers of the New Testament did not even mention the issue. Their silence was not because they were ignorant of the problem, and certainly not because they thought that it was acceptable, but because they were not going to waste their time flailing at the branches—they were putting their ax to the root of the tree, which was sin and estrangement from God. When people are reconciled to God, abortion and every other evil will be dealt with.

Jonathan Edwards, who was used to ignite the First Great Awakening, preached an anointed sermon, "Sinners in the Hands of an Angry God," that accomplished far more for the morality of this country than all the laws that were on the books at that time. All of the morality laws combined could not accomplish what the Great Awakenings did. Protests and demonstrations can have a place in a democratic society, but the church has a much higher calling. The church's authority is not found in the power to demonstrate, but in demonstrations of power.

Leo Tolstoy, possibly the greatest novelist who ever lived, once said: "Prophecy is like a spark lit in a dry wood. Once it ignites it will burn and burn until all of the wood, hay and stubble has been consumed." He gave as an example the history of slavery. This had been an accepted institution until believers began to clearly articulate, under the anointing, that it was wrong. Then it spread like fire lit in the dry wood. Within just a few years, the world was aflame with this truth, and slavery, at least in its most blatant forms, was quickly abolished throughout the earth.

One of the great sparks thrown on the dry wood of slavery was Harriet Beecher Stowe's novel, *Uncle Tom's Cabin*. This novel so clearly revealed the evils of slavery that it became impossible for that evil to abide any longer in the civilized world. When Abraham Lincoln met Mrs. Stowe during the Civil War, he exclaimed, "So you're the little lady that started this great war!" She was.

One of the greatest demonstrations of prophetic power in the church age came through Martin Luther. Luther was just a monk, but when he nailed his Ninety-Five Theses to the door of the tiny little church in the obscure town of Wittenburg, Germany, the whole world changed! Not only did he change the world in his own generation, but he also set in motion changes that have profoundly impacted every generation since. There has never been an emperor, king, or even a dynasty that has so influenced the world as this one monk.

Martin Luther is a profound testimony that even the most humble man who is armed with God's truth, and who refuses to compromise his convictions, is more powerful than armies. The power of Luther's prophetic stand is unequaled since the first century, when Paul and Silas caused the rulers of history's most powerful empire to tremble in fear, declaring in dismay, **"These who have turned the world upside down have come here too!" (Acts 17:6 NKJV)**

Mahatma Gandhi was said to have had a genuine conversion experience. However, he refused to be baptized when he saw how the event was being made a spectacle for the self-promotion of the evangelist. Nevertheless, he clung to many of the teachings of Jesus. He was especially captured by the Lord's admonition to overcome evil with good, and to turn the other cheek when assaulted. He determined to live by this code.

By focusing on just this one small part of the Lord's message, Gandhi was able to bring the most powerful empire of his day to its knees, giving birth to a nation. Gandhi refused to accept a political office, even though he could have easily been his nation's first prime minister. He simply stated that he had found a power greater than any power that a political office could ever give to him. He was right.

If Gandhi could so change his world by living by such a small fraction of the gospel, what kind of power would the church have if we all started to live by the whole gospel? If we really understood the power with which we have been entrusted, no pastor of a flock would ever care to stoop so low as to just become a president, much less a senator or congressman, unless it was a yoke clearly placed upon him by the Lord.

The Deadly Trap

One of the greatest traps set for those in spiritual authority is the temptation to use their influence in the realm of secular, civil authority. It is possible to use our influence to do good there, but good is the worst enemy of best. This is the same seduction that began in the Garden—the appeal to the positive aspects of the Tree of the Knowledge of Good and Evil. If we eat from that tree, we may be able to do a lot of "good," but in the end we, and the good that we have done, will perish.

Some have been called to serve in political positions, but it is clearly a delusion to call that a "high calling." It is in fact a very low calling as compared to a position of spiritual authority. When we have truly come to see who Jesus is, and who He has called us to be, we will have the constitution of Elijah, who could stand before the king and declare: **"As the LORD, the God of Israel lives, before whom I stand…"** (**I Kings 17:1**). By this, Elijah was saying to Ahab, "I am not standing here before you. You're just a king, just a man. I don't live my life before men; I live my life before the living God." When the church learns to likewise live before God rather than men, she will be entrusted with similar power.

Why should we even want to see a king, or president, or any other prominent person unless we have a divine mandate? We can go directly to the King of the universe anytime we want, with boldness. Why should we want to waste time trying to get legislation passed through the bizarre chaos of our legislatures? If we have seen the King in His glory, how can we even be impressed with presidents or kings from this earthly realm?

The Battle of Life

One of the great spiritual battles being waged by the church today is over abortion. The side that wins this conflict will have taken one of the truly important battles of our time, and it is right for the church to be fully engaged in this battle. However, if we "win" it in the wrong spirit, the consequences can be a defeat for the cause of the gospel.

If there is a greater revelation of the debauchery of humanity than what was revealed through the institution of slavery, it is abortion. Regardless of how many laws are passed legalizing this great evil, the laws of nature have already been passed. Nature itself reveals that abortion is probably the lowest level to which depraved humanity has yet fallen. Even the beasts will instinctively sacrifice their own lives to protect their young, but we have proven willing to sacrifice our children for the most petty reasons of convenience and selfishness. While we bemoan the whales and spotted owls, we massacre our own young, helpless, and innocent by the most cruel, torturous means.

This is a tragedy of epic proportions. How the church confronts this great evil can potentially result in one of her greatest victories, or result in even more lives being lost for eternity. Revival is usually God's final attempt to show mercy instead of judgment. The last of the Great Awakenings this country experienced came just before the Civil War. That awakening was given by the Lord as a way to prevent the Civil War. Had that revival continued on track, it would almost certainly have abolished slavery without the worst bloodshed this nation has ever experienced. When the revival was turned from its course by the political zealots of that time, the Abolitionists, the fate of the nation was sealed and bloodshed was inevitable.

The Abolitionists were some of the most courageous, truth loving, and self-sacrificing people in the country. Most were Christians, and true patriots. However, they were also driven to extremes and blown about by the winds of impatience. Their goals were noble, but their means were often destructive, because they did not comprehend the nature of the **"wisdom from above"** as described by James:

> **Who among you is wise and understanding? Let him show by his good behavior his deeds in the gentleness of wisdom.**

> **But the wisdom from above is first pure, then peaceable, gentle, reasonable, full of mercy and good fruits, unwavering, without hypocrisy.**

> **And the seed whose fruit is righteousness is sown in peace by those who make peace (James 3:13, 17-18).**

The Abolitionists had the right goals, but they sometimes tried to achieve them by the wrong means. Whenever we do this, we depart from the wisdom that is from above, and display a nature that is quite the opposite of the Savior's. Zealotry is the wisdom of Judas Iscariot, who thought that he could force the Lord to take His authority and declare His kingdom. Such political manipulation comes from the spirit of the evil one, regardless of the motives of those who use it. The kingdom of God will not come that way.

One of the ultimate choices now facing the church is if we want our political goals accomplished or the kingdom of God to come. John Brown (of the famous "John Brown's Raid") is considered by many, including himself, to have been a prophet. There are many with this same spirit moving throughout the church today, which will pressure others to act prematurely and to use carnal weapons to assault spiritual fortresses. They exert this pressure with the argument that "so many babies are being lost each day." This is a truth that should weigh on us, but their means will not result in any fewer babies being aborted, and their tactics can ultimately lead to more bloodshed than we can now comprehend.

Whenever spiritual men have tried to establish authority or influence in the civil realm of authority, without being called to such a position, they have almost always become extremists who damaged their own cause. Those who fall to this trap are usually the most zealous for the Lord and His purposes, but zeal without humble submission to the Holy Spirit will inevitably become a useful tool of the enemy.

If Satan finds someone whom he cannot stop, he will then try to push them too far. Unfortunately, this is often very easy with the zealot. As soon as the enemy is able to push people into a realm where they have not been called, beyond the grace that they have been given, he can use them as effective weapons in his hand.

We must stop expecting the government to do our job. The Lord hears prayer, and He has more power than the President, Congress, and the Supreme

Court combined! The issue of abortion has the power to divide this country as it has not been divided since the Civil War. Prayer can bring a revival that can prevent this. Such a revival, if it is not sidetracked by zealots, will have the power to abolish abortion and replace it with the greatest esteem for life that civilization has yet realized.

God's History Book

The Book of Life is God's history book, and it paints a very different picture from human histories. In God's history, many of the great heroes were men and women that were "unknowns" in the world, but these praying saints had authority with God and accomplished much more for the human race than any president, prime minister, or king ever did. Praying saints have freed many more slaves than Wilberforce and Lincoln combined—and the freedom that they brought about was much greater! This is why the Lord said in Luke 10:18-20:

> **"I was watching Satan fall from heaven like lightning.**
>
> **"Behold, I have given you authority to tread upon serpents and scorpions, and over all the power of the enemy, and nothing shall injure you.**
>
> **"Nevertheless do not rejoice in this, that the spirits are subject to you, but rejoice that your names are recorded in heaven."**

It is a wonderful thing to have been given authority **"over all of the power of the enemy,"** but it is an even greater thing to be found in God's history book—the Book of Life. The way that we make it into His history book is to live by the authority of His Book, without succumbing to the temptation to live by human authority. What good will it do us to be known by all men, but not to be known by God? It is much better to have influence with God than to have influence with all men. Let us again hear the warning Jesus gave to us:

> **"Not everyone who says to Me, 'Lord, Lord,' will enter the kingdom of heaven; but he who does the will of My Father who is in heaven.**
>
> **"Many will say to Me on that day, 'Lord, Lord, did we not prophesy in Your name, and in Your name cast out demons, and in Your name perform many miracles?'**
>
> **"And then I will declare to them, 'I never knew you; depart from Me, you who practice lawlessness'" (Matthew 7:21-23).**

Chapter Thirteen
The Battle for Life and Liberty

In nature, the preservation of life is the most basic and powerful motivation. Because of this, except in only a few of the most primitive species, family is a primary drive of life. It was no accident that the very first test of Solomon's wisdom was concerning the issue of a mother's devotion to her child's life. The very first test of wisdom for any government is likewise its commitment to the sanctity of life.

Just because something is legal does not make it right. There are fundamental laws that prevail in nature which reveal a great deal more wisdom than politicians have been able to display. True morality is not dictated simply by legal compliance; true morality is doing what is right.

A civilization that is not based on law will be open to despotism and tyranny. But a civilization that cannot rise above the law to live by what is not just legal, but what is also moral, has lost its humanity and its potential for true greatness. Lawlessness always results in tyranny. The inability to rise above law will also result in tyranny. The preservation of life is fundamental to both nature and morality.

Parents who sacrifice their offspring would have difficulty finding acceptance even in the animal kingdom. There will be no peace of mind or peace on earth until life is esteemed above selfish ambition or convenience. It is not only unnatural for a mother to destroy her child, born or unborn, but it reveals a fundamental departure from civilization to embrace a barbarism in its most base and inhumane form.

The resolution of the abortion issue gives us the opportunity to provide the world leadership in finding even higher standards of morality, justice, and the esteem for life. The failure to resolve it with courage and honor, not just with law, will certainly leave a major crack in our foundations, which must ultimately lead to tyranny of the most frightening kind.

Arenas of the Battle for Life

As stated, there is no question that the church should be involved in the battle for life, whether it deals with abortion, euthanasia, or other issues such as some that are being raised in the field of biochemistry. The issue is under what sphere of authority we will address them, and whether we will compromise the authority that we have been given by trying to do the right thing in the wrong realm.

Spiritual authority comes from the Holy Spirit, and He is the Spirit of Truth. He will only endorse with His authority those who are true, who live what they preach. Can we cast stones at the mother who aborts her child if we are sacrificing our living children at the altars of the petty gods of selfish ambition and personal success? Could even the greatest success of our enterprises be interpreted as anything but a terrible human failure if we lose the souls of our own children in the process?

Who can count the "successful" Christian businessmen, sportsmen, coaches, and even church leaders, who have accomplished their goals only to say that they would trade everything just to have their families back? The first condition that God said was not good, was for man to be alone—and that is exactly where we will end up if we do not give our families the priority they deserve.

Spiritual Abortion

In 1989, I had an experience in which I was caught up into the presence of the Lord. In this experience I was a witness to the Lord's anger over abortion. To my surprise, His anger was directed at the church and not the heathen. He declared that if the church had not aborted the spiritual seeds that He had planted in her— for missions, outreaches, and even simple witnessing to our neighbors—then the unsaved would not be living in such darkness and would not be aborting their natural seed.

In this vision, God said that the church was aborting His spiritual seed for all the same reasons that the heathen were aborting their unborn—because of our selfishness, because these "children" (converts) would be expensive and we did not think we could afford them, and because we did not want to give them our time. He affirmed that judgment would come upon our country because of the evil of abortion, but that He was going to start with His own household first!

How many teenage girls would not need abortions now if we had responded to the Holy Spirit when He impressed us to witness to them? It is time for us to quit flailing at the branches and put the ax to the root of the tree! Abortion is a great evil, but it is just one of the symptoms of the terrible disease of humanity—sin.

Abortion must be stopped, but it is now far beyond the government's ability to stop it. That doesn't excuse the government from trying, but the only thing that can stop abortion in this country now is a revival on the level of another Great Awakening. As a believer, I will give the majority of my attention to obedience, prayer, and seeking revival. In a revival atmosphere, effective laws can be passed that will help against this evil, just as Finney's revivals helped to spark our government's actions against slavery. Without revival, the same laws would be useless—the people will simply break the laws on a scale that the government can do little about.

If the church is going to accomplish anything of significance—concerning abortion or any other issue—she must repent of her own sins, and then realize the Source of her power. To repeat Paul's statement, "**...We are ready to punish all disobedience, whenever your obedience is complete**" **(II Corinthians 10:6).** When our obedience is complete, we will then have the authority to deal with "**all disobedience**" in our society, but it will not be mainly with political demonstrations, but with demonstrations of power, which are able to accomplish far more.

The Stronghold of Homosexuality

If we believe that the Bible is God's Word, we must understand that homosexuality is sin and must be dealt with as sin. So we must ask the question: Should the church tolerate sin? That is a pretty sticky issue. Most of us are still struggling with some problems that would have to fall under the sin category. Strife and outbursts of anger are listed right along with immorality, idolatry, and sorcery as works of the flesh in Galatians 5:19-21. If we tried to remove everyone from the church who had a problem with anger, there would probably not be many people left.

However, the Lord did not call every sin in the Bible an "abomination" and "perversion" like He did homosexuality (see Leviticus 20:13). The Lord only named those sins abominations that were especially repulsive to Him, or that were especially corrupting and destructive to society. Homosexuality falls into such a category. The Lord destroyed Sodom for this sin, and there is clearly a point at which the Lord will judge a nation for the spread of this sin, because of its corrupting influence.

In Romans 1:26 Paul called homosexuality a sin **"against nature,"** and he promised that those who practiced it would receive in their bodies the **"penalty of their error" (verse 27 NKJV)**. AIDS is an obvious example of this penalty. Biblically, we can see that most plagues have their origin in the spirit, as the result of widespread sin. The characteristics of the plague usually reflect the sin that has released it.

AIDS is a virus that causes the destruction of the immune system, or the body's defenses. Homosexuality and other forms of perversion are the primary causes of the release of AIDS, and those sins do destroy a society's defenses against evil in all forms. Homosexuality thus is a particularly potent "gate of hell."

God Loves Gays

So how should the church respond to homosexuals? Love them! We should love them because God does, **"who desires all men to be saved and to come to the knowledge of the truth" (I Timothy 2:4)**. God loves homosexuals and desires their salvation. God is love, and even His judgment, through plagues or other means, is a result of His love—it is His last call to repentance that they might be saved. The church will not have any true authority over this problem until she loves those with the problem. When we get into shouting matches with gays, we are only multiplying the very demon we are seeking to cast out.

Does this mean that we should just open our churches, our schools, and our families to the influence of homosexuals? No. Homosexuality is a genuine threat to the very foundations of our social order, and it will become an increasingly blatant threat to our religious liberty, which poses the greatest threat to their particular sin.

However, Satan will not cast out Satan. If our confrontation with this sin is not in the right spirit, then we are actually multiplying the power of the evil we are seeking to cast out. This may come as a shock, but the church must also repent of her part in being a major cause for the release of homosexuality in society.

Homosexuality and Worship

One cause of the growing release of homosexuality in society is the increasing departure from true worship. People were created to be worshipers. If they are not devoted to the proper worship of the Creator, they will fall to worshiping the creation, which Paul explained in the first chapter of Romans to be the cause of homosexuality.

Music and other forms of art were talents given to men and women so they could express their adoration of God. Using our spiritual gifts, or natural talents, in adoration of God is the highest form of fulfillment we can know on this earth. Yet many of the most gifted artists in history were homosexuals. Many of these fell to homosexuality because there was no outlet in the church for their worship through the arts. Therefore, they turned to worshiping the creation instead of the Creator. Homosexuals who are delivered from their sin and given a proper outlet for the gifts God has given to them will become some of the purest worshipers of the Lord, and will help to release true worship in the church.

This is not to imply that the entire problem of homosexuality is the result of the church being closed to certain forms of worship through the arts. The bulk of the depravity is simply the choice of people to worship the creature rather than the Creator. However, since the church is called to be the light of the world, if the world is falling into increasing darkness, we should not blame it on the government, or even society, but on the church. The answers to society's problems are spiritual, not political. When we seek to combat social and moral problems, we must do more than condemn and alienate people—we must have the truth that sets them free.

Homo-sect-uality

There is a "spiritual homosexuality" from which the church must be delivered if we are going to have spiritual authority over this sin. Spiritual homosexuality is having relationships only with your own kind, which is sectarianism.

A root of homosexuality is the fear of rejection, which pushes one toward isolation and the compulsion to stay away from those who are different. Men and women represent the ultimate human differences, and almost everyone has to overcome the fear of rejection in order to cross the bridge to a relationship with the other sex. The same is true in the church: It is the insecurity of much of the leadership that causes them to refrain from any kind of relationship with those who are different. This results in sectarianism, which is a subtle form of spiritual homosexuality.

An important key to helping bring deliverance to one who is in the bondage of homosexuality is not to reject them, but to love and accept them—not their sin, but them. **"Perfect love casts out fear" (see I John 4:18),** and fear is one of the primary things that holds them in bondage.

One of the remarkable characteristics of the Lord's own ministry, which is to be the model for all true ministry, is that He was the friend of sinners. Not only did He feel comfortable around them, but even more amazing, they felt comfortable around Him. Jesus did not condemn sinners; He changed them by loving them. This is not to imply that He did not challenge their sin, but He did it with genuine love. This enabled Him to share the truth that would set them free, not just heap more burdens on them.

We must learn to treat sinners the way Jesus did, with open arms and the answers to their problems. The answer is not to alienate them further, but to reach out to them with genuine love and help. This requires remembering that the majority are not like the extreme caricatures we have often made them into, just as most Christians are not like the caricatures made of us.

Can a Christian Be a Liberal?

There are many sincere Christians who are political liberals. Unfortunately, this is usually because they see more genuine caring for the poor and the oppressed among liberals than they do among conservative Christians. Some politicians have stated that when they see Christians caring more for the needy than the liberals do, they will start listening to the church more than to the liberals.

Winston Churchill once said: "If a man is not a liberal when he is twenty, he has no heart. If he is not a conservative when he is forty, he has no mind." Most Christians agree with liberals that we must take care of the needy and the oppressed, but disagree with the premise that the government should, or even could, do it.

There are some people who really do need charity, and will need it their entire lives. As the Lord said, **"for the poor you have with you always..." (Matthew 26:11).** It is not realistic to think that poverty will be eradicated before the kingdom comes.

We must also recognize that poor people are an opportunity for us to love and help others, and it is a great privilege to be able to do so. But when we try to do this through the government, it becomes depersonalized and institutionalized. Most government programs are so bogged down in waste and inefficiency that only a fraction of the resources actually reaches the needs of the people. But this is not just a problem with the government. When any charity becomes institutionalized, it has a way of dehumanizing the people and perpetuating a dependency on the institution. Many times the attempted cure for society's ills has proven worse than the disease.

The church and the needy have both greatly suffered from the church's recent tendency to relinquish its role in serving the poor, or establishing moral standards, to the government. The whole trend toward the government trying to be the answer for all of society's problems is based on the failure of the church to live up to her mandate. The government is likely to continue degenerating into socialistic delusions until the church stands up to do her job. The answer to every human problem is found at the cross. The answer to every human need is found in Christ. Until the church lifts Him up, the world will continue living in darkness and delusion.

Summary

The church has had a long history of trying to bring the kingdom of God to earth by her own might and power, without the Spirit. But the Lord stated: **"That which is born of the flesh is flesh, and that which is born of the Spirit is spirit" (John 3:6).** Even if we are trying to accomplish the right goal, if it is not done by the Holy Spirit, we will end up wounding instead of healing, bringing further division instead of reconciliation.

The historic church, called to carry the gospel of salvation to the world, has been responsible for some of the deepest wounds that mankind has suffered. Inevitably, the roots of these tragic mistakes can be traced to the same error—well-intentioned people trying to use the civil realm of authority to accomplish spiritual goals.

Whenever people have tried to bring down spiritual strongholds with carnal weapons, it has only resulted in a terrible defeat for the gospel. Such efforts will always fall into using another spirit to accomplish the purposes of God, which results in the spiritual strongholds of the enemy being made even stronger, regardless of the political consequences.

The whole world is very aware of this history of the church. It seems that only the church is ignorant of her history, so each new generation has stumbled into the same traps. Regardless of how painful it is, we must examine our history and judge the fruit of the methods and teachings that we continue to repeat.

Contrary to popular belief, time does not heal wounds; they will only heal if they are dressed and closed. The terrible wounds inflicted upon Muslims and Jews by the Crusades remain open, and have become increasingly infected with the passage of time.

The reason that the sins of the fathers are passed on to the children, generation after generation, is not to punish the children for what their fathers have done. However, until a generation arises to repent of the sins, addressing and bringing closure to the wounds, the sins will continue to be perpetuated. This is why the leaders of restoration movements in Scripture, such as Ezra and Nehemiah, gave so much attention to addressing and repenting for the sins of their spiritual fathers in previous generations.

The enemy, knowing the power of the church when she devotes herself to the ministry of reconciliation, continually tries to divert her from this commission. So far he has been very successful at using this tactic, and every new movement has somehow allowed the same seeds of its ultimate destruction to be sown. Churches, denominations, movements, and even individuals are still trying to conquer by might and power rather than by the Spirit—and every such "crusade" only results in more wounds.

It is true that there were many historic atrocities inflicted upon Christians by Muslims, and even by some Jews, but that is not our problem. Regardless of what was done by others, our mistakes were the most tragic of all, because they were done in the name of the Savior who had come to deliver people from such evil.

For the church to accomplish her last-day mandate, we do not need public opinion, force of numbers, financial resources, or political power—we need the grace of God. Because God gives His grace to the humble, we must learn to take every opportunity that we get to humble ourselves. One of the primary ways that the church can do this is to acknowledge our historic mistakes, asking forgiveness from those that we have so tragically persecuted and wounded. Such humility has an extraordinary power to tear down the barriers and walls that separate people and cultures, and to release the ministry of reconciliation.

This powerful weapon of humility was demonstrated by Jesus on the cross, when He suffered the worst humiliation that the ruthless powers of this world could muster against Him, for the sake of the very ones who tortured Him. In His most agonizing moment, He did not ask for retaliation—He asked for His tormentors to be forgiven. By the power released through His humility, He overcame the world, and was exalted to a position above all powers and authorities.

The Scriptures are clear that in the final days of this age the church will be exalted to a spiritual position of authority she has never experienced before, which she must attain to accomplish her last-day mandate. The path to that great exaltation is humility. Only when she has been properly humbled can she be trusted with this great authority.

From the time that there were just two brothers, Cain and Abel, people have not been able to get along, and murder has gripped the fallen human heart. Until true redemption prevails, war will be with us. On that terrible day when the Crusaders took Jerusalem, Satan obviously saw one of the best chances that he would ever have to defame the glorious name of Jesus, and he took full advantage of it.

The Lord is now looking for a generation that will live by another spirit, the Holy Spirit. This new generation of believers will humble themselves and pray, seeking His face and turning from their wicked ways. Then the Lord will hear from heaven and heal our land.

When this healing has reached Jerusalem, touching the heart of the Jew with the grace and truth that is realized through Jesus Christ, it will mark the completion of the great work of this church age. Then we will know that the bride has come of age, and the spots have been removed.

Chapter Fourteen

Twelve Lessons on Warfare

S ome events which take place in the natural realm
reflect important spiritual principles. The Persian
Gulf War was such an event. The strategies that
were implemented in this war to secure victory are
comparable to those which will enable us to be victori-
ous in spiritual warfare. This chapter is not meant to
imply a certain political view or justification for the
Persian Gulf War, but simply uses that war as an illustration of important principles of spiritual warfare.

Principle Number 1: We Must Clearly Define Our Objectives

Possibly the greatest contributing factor to the
Allied victory in the Persian Gulf War was the resolve
of the leadership to hold their course and not compromise their objectives. It is improbable that such
resolve could have been maintained without clearly
defined objectives, which stood like a fortress
against the political maneuvering and pressure

before, during, and after the war. Until we, the church, clearly understand our objectives for this hour, it is improbable that we will ever accomplish what we have been given to do.

The Allies did not begin the battle without a mandate from the United Nations. Of course, the church does not get our mandate from the United Nations, but we do need a mandate from the Lord before we begin. The church is presently made up of many "nations," or "denomi-nations" and movements.

Principle Number 2: The Greater the Unity, the Greater the Victory

What the United States leadership did to secure the unanimous approval of the United Nations' resolutions, and then forge a coalition of such diverse nations to fight the battle, offers a penetrating illustration of exactly what is required for the church to win against schemes of our enemy. We are told that the gates of hell will not prevail against the church (see Matthew 16:18). Notice here that the Lord did not say "churches," but "church"—singular.

The gates of hell are the enemy's access points into our lives, our congregations, our cities, and our nations. The church has the authority to shut those gates. They cannot prevail against the church, singular, but they will continue to prevail against a church divided. If the Syrians, Egyptians, Saudi Arabians, Americans, French, British, and others could join under one command to fight Saddam, then certainly the Baptists, Methodists, Lutherans, Pentecostals, Charismatics, Catholics, etc., should be able to unify to wage our war against Satan.

The Allied coalition did not require the Syrians to become Americans or British, or to give up their sovereignty in any way. Neither is the church required to come under a single human organization or authority. History contains a resounding testimony to the terrible fallacy of the church coming under any head but Jesus. But there are common purposes that we must rally around if there is to be victory. Many of the different camps within the church have become so afraid of losing their domain that they have been giving territory to the enemy in order to keep their brothers from getting too much! In order to escape excessive authority, we have often chosen anarchy.

If the church is to have victory in our time, we, too, must learn to join coalitions which confront specific issues, with specific objectives, until those objectives are fully accomplished. This will mean laying aside the fears of pastors and leaders who make sure their meetings are so ambiguous that nothing is accomplished.

At the risk of offending other world leaders and powers, the United States took the initiative and the leadership to get the job done. Instead of bringing the feared division, that initiative and resolve brought the most improbable coalition into a unity which accomplished an astonishingly one-sided victory. It is time for those who have been anointed as leaders to take the initiative to forge the coalitions needed to win spiritual battles in their cities and nations.

Principle Number 3: When It Is Time to Fight, We Must Not Hesitate

When we receive the commission, we cannot be timid. If the time to fight comes and we do not fight, the "paralysis of analysis" will quickly set in. We will then be defeated by default, through our own indecision.

Just as some have sought to use antiwar movements to derail our nation's resolve in battle, there is a very subtle spiritual antiwar movement that the enemy would use to derail the church's resolve in spiritual warfare. The spiritual antiwar movement stems from a misguided idealism.

Idealism is the root of humanism; it is the "good" side of the Tree of the Knowledge of Good and Evil, and its fruit is just as deadly as that of the evil side of that same tree. In addition to idealism, the spiritual antiwar movement is based on a subtle fear of the enemy. However, it is not biblical for us to fear the enemy; the only one we are to fear is the Lord. As if to specifically address this problem, the Lord stated clearly: **"Behold, I have given you authority to tread upon serpents and scorpions, and over all the power of the enemy, and nothing shall injure you"** (Luke 10:19).

The rallying cry for the antiwar movement during the Persian Gulf War became "no blood for oil." Oil is energy, or power. It is a biblical practice for us to anoint with oil, because this oil represents the energy or power of the Holy Spirit.

It is most interesting that the cry of the antiwar movement would be "no blood for oil," because that is exactly contrary to reality. Both in the natural and in the spiritual, if we were not willing to fight for that most strategic region, the primary energy source of the whole world would soon have been in the control of some of history's cruelest and most irrational despots. The price that we would then have had to pay for oil would have been our freedom. Islam means "submission," and world dominion is a foundation of their religion. If we had not fought when we did, we would have ended up submitting to them later.

The same is true in the spirit; there is no anointing (oil) without sacrifice. It was by the blood of Jesus that the anointing of the Holy Spirit was given. It is through taking up our crosses daily to follow Him that we are able to walk in this anointing. When we lay aside the cross and the blood, we lose the oil.

Just as the most contested region of the world is the location of the greatest oil reserves, the same is true in the spirit. Where the greatest controversies are currently found in the body of Christ is precisely where the greatest anointing is usually found. If we do not fight for those areas, we will lose the oil!

Principle Number 4: We Must Choose Our Leaders Carefully, and Then Let Them Lead

We can have the best troops in the world, equipped with the best weapons, but if they are poorly led, we will probably be defeated. Many of the great and strategic battles in history were lost simply because the military leaders were chosen for political reasons. This mistake was not made in the Gulf War, and that is one of the reasons for its extraordinary success.

President George Bush may have been the commander in chief, but he was not a military strategist, and he knew it. To his credit, he laid out the overall objective, to which the Allies agreed, and then he let the generals do their job without interfering. Saddam Hussein failed at this point.

Someone can be a great leader of people in one area, and yet be a very poor leader in another. However, it is usually difficult for leaders to understand this. For example, it is hard for pastors or leaders of ministries to refrain from getting too involved in the details of every program, outreach, or ministry. This is one of the greatest millstones to which such programs or ministries are often subjected. It is the reason for many of our defeats.

Principle Number 5: The Air War Must Be Implemented First

This speaks of the fact that the war has to be fought in the heavenlies first, through intercession, before we implement the "ground assault." Failure to do this will result in many unnecessary casualties. The low cost, in terms of casualties, of the Allied victory over Iraq was directly related to the patience and success of the air war.

The initial targets of the air war were the enemy's communications, radar, nuclear and chemical warfare facilities, and missile launchers. These should likewise be the first targets of our prayers—the enemy's evil communications (what he is using to accuse, slander, and malign the brethren), the sources he is using to generate poison (bitterness, jealousy, etc.), and what he is using to launch his **"fiery darts"** (missiles) at believers (see Ephesians 6:16 NKJV).

Principle Number 6: We Must Not Succumb to the Scud Missile Diversion

It is significant that the Iraqi "Scud" missiles were almost able to sidetrack the Allied strategy. Large numbers of planes and missions were diverted to locate the Scud missile launchers, even though it was admitted that the Scuds were "purely political and psychological weapons with no real military value."

Scud missiles appropriately represent criticism. Criticism can do a little political and psychological damage, but it really cannot hurt us strategically unless we let it divert us from our course. Many churches, ministries, and movements in history have been thrown off their courses by such Scud missiles that were not really doing any serious damage. We must not overreact to the Scud missiles that the enemy launches, since they are purely political and psychological; we must keep our resources directed at the targets that are of true "military" value.

Principle Number 7: Our Weapons Must Be Precise

One striking characteristic of the Allied air assault was the precision of the weapons. This is an issue we must understand in our intercession. We must know exactly what our targets are, and must be able to hit them with precision.

The Apostle Paul said that we do not box **"as one who beats the air"** (see **I Corinthians 9:26 NKJV**). One of the first things a boxer learns is that when he swings and misses he will expend far more energy than when he hits his opponent. When we just flail away at principalities and powers that we do not understand, we are exhausting ourselves to the point where the enemy can then throw an easy knockout punch at us. Spiritual warfare will be effective only to the degree that we have specific targets, and that our weapons are precise.

"For the weapons of our warfare are not carnal, but mighty through God to the pulling down of strongholds" (II Corinthians 10:4 KJV). If we are properly using the weapons that we have been given, there will be strongholds brought down. Every year, we should be able to see strongholds conquered in our personal lives. Each congregation should be able to point to strongholds in its community that have been brought down. Movements and denominations that have been given authority on a national or international basis should be able to point to specific strongholds on that level that have been brought down, or are in the process of crumbling.

If we really have the authority that we say we do, where's the fruit? Why are we not getting results? One thing that we can be sure of, the problem is not with the weapons that we have been given. For some reason they are either not being used or they are being used improperly.

Principle Number 8: There Must Be Specialization in Missions

Another relevant characteristic of the Allied air strategy is that different types of aircraft were used for different types of missions. The Stealth fighters attacked the enemy radar; the British had aircraft with weapons specially designed to destroy enemy runways; F-111's attacked missile bunkers, and nuclear and chemical facilities; B-52's carpet-bombed enemy fortifications; F-14's provided air cover protection from enemy fighters, etc.

The body of Christ must come to this same type of specialization and coordination of its ministries if we are going to be effective in our purpose. Presently we have evangelists trying to be pastors, pastors trying to be prophets, prophets trying to be teachers, etc. Not only are we ineffective when we try to function outside of the calling that we have been given, but we are also hindering the one who was called to that place.

Even the most talented sports team would have little chance of victory if the players decided that they were going to play the position that they wanted to play without regard to the coach's strategy or the game plan. Likewise, the church has little hope of victory until we learn basic teamwork.

Principle Number 9: One of the Greatest Dangers Will Be from Friendly Fire

In the Persian Gulf War, the United States possibly had more casualties from "friendly fire" than from the enemy. These were accidents caused either by a lack of coordination or a failure to identify whether a target was "friend or foe" before firing. This problem was usually caused by the fear and confusion of battle.

Casualties from friendly fire are obviously a problem in the church as well. Far more damage to the church is caused by Christians attacking each other than by the hand of the enemy. Often this, too, is simply a lack of coordination and the failure to communicate. Others just start firing at other Christians before they have taken the time to identify if they are friend or foe.

Just as in the Persian Gulf War, friendly fire in the church is usually caused by insecurity or confusion. However, there is no excuse for these within the church. We are called to walk by faith, not by fear. If we are allowing fear or confusion to control us, then we are already firmly in the hands of the enemy, and we will be used by him against our own people.

Principle Number 10: We Must Be Patient Before Beginning the Ground War, but There Will Be No Victory Without It

Until the enemy has been bound in heaven, he will not be bound on earth. Only that which has been loosed in heaven can be loosed on the earth. Evangelism and church planting is our ground war, and they will be far more effective when we learn to accomplish all that can be accomplished in the air first, with strategic intercession. Even so, the war will not be won until there is an effective ground assault. It will not happen with prayer alone; we must also preach the gospel, building people into temples that the Lord can inhabit, who then will take prophetic stands for the truth.

When we send evangelists into the harvest fields, we should be sending pastors and teachers behind them to hold the ground that is taken. Casting principalities down is not enough; they must be displaced. The light must overcome the darkness. Salvation is the beginning, but our calling is to **"make disciples... teaching them to observe all"** that the Lord commanded us **(see Matthew 28:19-20)**. The true New Testament convert is one who is added to the church, not just one who makes a "decision."

When the ground war begins, the air war does not stop, but it does change its strategy. When the ground assault begins, much of the air force becomes subject to the ground forces, which call for attacks on specific targets. Evangelists and church planters who go into the field should have the same kind of communication with intercessory prayer teams, giving them specific directives for prayer.

> **For we do not wrestle against flesh and blood, but against principalities, against powers, against the rulers of the darkness of this age, against spiritual hosts of wickedness in the heavenly places (Ephesians 6:12 NKJV).**

Wrestling is the very closest form of combat. There is not true spiritual warfare if there is no encounter with the enemy. The ones whom we are called to wrestle against are not low level demons, but principalities and powers. Paul exhorted the Ephesians: **"Finally, be strong in the Lord, and in the strength of His might. Put on the full armor of God, that you may be able to stand firm against the schemes of the devil" (Ephesians 6:10-11).** This is a very real conflict, and it must be waged with the utmost seriousness, responsibility, and care or there will be much unnecessary loss.

Principle Number 11: We Must Not Stop Fighting Until the Victory Is Complete

The Gulf War coalition was certainly blessed with wisdom and strategy, but there was one flaw in the plan that could yet prove costly. Iraq was not the enemy—it was Saddam Hussein. Strategically, removing Saddam from power should have been as much of a goal as defeating his army.

This is not meant to be a political comment on the Gulf War, or the righteousness or unrighteousness of it. However, it is a historic fact that when a nation is defeated in war, but its leader is not removed from power, he will very likely have to be fought again. The church has been very guilty of this same folly. We will gain a measure of victory and then back off before the enemy is utterly defeated. We, therefore, end up needlessly fighting the same battles over and over.

When the king of Israel came to Elisha to ask if he should go to battle with the Syrians, the prophet told him to take his bow and arrows and strike the ground (see II Kings 13:14-19). The king did as he requested, and struck the ground three times. The prophet was angry, and scolded the king for only striking the ground three times, which meant that he would only defeat his enemy three times. There are prophetic events such as this, which can have much greater consequences than the natural mind can comprehend. Even so, we must learn to take our weapons and strike over and over until the enemy is utterly destroyed, or we will have to fight the same enemy again.

When the biblical nation of Israel failed to utterly destroy her enemies, those enemies returned to defeat her. The same has been historically true with the church. In spiritual warfare there can be no truce with the enemy. When we fight for our inheritance, we must do what Joshua did before the city of Ai: **"For Joshua did not withdraw his hand with which he stretched out the javelin until he had utterly destroyed all the inhabitants of Ai"** (Joshua 8:26).

We are not warring with flesh and blood, but against principalities and powers, which the biblical enemies of Israel represented (see Ephesians 6:12). We have to learn to extend the javelin until the enemy is utterly destroyed. How many times have we allowed our enemies to escape to fight us another day, because when we got a measure of victory, we let up? This has been a most repetitive and tragic mistake of the church.

Principle Number 12: After the Victory, We Must Beware of Those Who Try to Join Us with Stale Bread and Old Wineskins

After Joshua's victory at Ai, the Gibeonites came to him with stale bread and old wineskins, claiming to be from a far country (see Joshua 9). Joshua made a covenant with them without seeking the Lord. Israel would pay for this impetuous mistake for generations.

One of our most vulnerable times is immediately following a great victory. We tend to let down our guard, and a subtle pride slips in. Pride indeed comes before a fall (see Proverbs 16:18). That is why Paul warned us: **"Therefore let him who thinks he stands take heed lest he fall"** (I Corinthians 10:12).

The euphoria that accompanies victory can cause us to be generous with our enemy, which he will consistently use to his own advantage. After the victory is when we will be in the greatest jeopardy of making unholy alliances. Everyone tries to join a winner, and few who are in the euphoric state of victory can discern the origin of those who are seeking to join them. An unholy alliance can ultimately prove to be more destructive than having lost the battle. Holy alliances, on the other hand, are usually made when the outcome of the battle is still uncertain; that is when we find those who are really committed to the cause.

The Mohican Indians forfeited their future because they made a wrong alliance, choosing to fight with the British during the Revolutionary War. Many nations have done the same throughout history. So have many churches, movements, and denominations. Spiritual alliances are sometimes powerful vehicles for the advancement of the gospel, but we should never make an alliance with anyone without a clear leading from the Lord.

Summary

Although this book has addressed some of the most powerful evil strongholds of these last days, and the biblical strategy for confronting them, it simply is not possible to comprehensively address these subjects in a single volume. I realize that I have probably left as many questions as I have provided answers, but that, too, was part of my purpose.

Questions will stir a true seeker to find answers. There are many others now addressing some of these same issues, and I trust some are doing it with greater depth and understanding. I am trying to point in the basic direction that we need to follow, rather than trying to offer final conclusions.

I do have two follow-up volumes already planned for this series. The main purpose of the follow-up books will be to address other large, general strongholds. Most of these have personal applications. The illumination of these strongholds can help us to become free of our own yokes, and that is essential before we will ever have authority over principalities and powers in the heavenly places.

Much of the understanding that I have come to in these matters is because of the grip that they once had in my own life, or in some cases still do to a degree. Even so, I never want to settle for less than a complete deliverance, and hope to one day stand with the truth as a full victor over these great strongholds. This is the calling and destiny of the last day church.

It is true that the present church seems very far from being such a victor over evil. The Saturday edition of many newspapers in the United States has a section for churches to advertise their Sunday morning programs. A friend of mine likes to read the headlines first, and then go to this section to see how well the church is relating to the pressing issues of the day. To date, this has been a very disheartening exercise, as the church seems almost completely out of step with the times.

I have listened to some "cutting edge" teachings on such subjects as leadership and church growth. Many of these are outstanding teachings, but since I have come from a business background, I recognize many of them as decades old principles borrowed from the business world. Although I have no problem with some of these being taught in the church, my greatest regret is that what is so often new and fresh to the church is so far behind the world.

Those who are the closest to the Creator should be far ahead of the world in creativity. Those who are closest to the King of kings should be far ahead of the world in leadership. The church is called to be the head, not the tail (see Deuteronomy 28:13). We are called to be a thermostat, not a thermometer. The first-century church was so creative that she constantly shocked and befuddled her enemies. The world could not stop the church, because the world was always so far behind her. It was not until the church settled into her boring and predictable patterns that the world caught up, and then overtook her.

If the church is to have any relevance to these times, she must begin to walk in prophetic vision that both sees and walks in the power of the age to come. We must stop attempting to reach the world by trying to keep up with it—we must press beyond the limits of our time and seize the future with boldness.

If we are going to win this battle of the ages, we must go beyond just knowing the future; we must set its course. True, biblical, sanctified, dynamic creativity must be recovered in the church if we are to have any hope of being relative to these times. The church, born so vibrant and spontaneous, will rise again. The world that now yawns at the church is about to be shocked by a people who arise with so much life that even the dead will be raised by their touch.

The River of Life is coming to His church. This River is going to overflow all of its present banks. None of the dikes erected to keep it in place will be able to restrain what is coming. No stronghold can stand before this River. You are called to be a part of it, and no evil will stand before you as you flow with Him.

Other Books by Rick Joyner

The Overcoming Life

The Power to Change the World

A Message to the Glorious Church, Vol. I

A Message to the Glorious Church, Vol. II

The Apostolic Ministry

Delivered From Evil

Overcoming Evil in the Last Days

Breaking the Power of Evil

Leadership: The Power of a Creative Life

A Prophetic Vision for the 21st Century

The Final Quest

The Call

The Torch and the Sword

There Were Two Trees in the Garden

The Journey Begins

The Surpassing Greatness of His Power

The Prophetic Ministry

50 Days for an Enduring Vision

50 Days for a Soaring Vision

50 Days for a Firm Foundation

The World Aflame

Hall of Faith Series

Combating Spiritual Strongholds Series

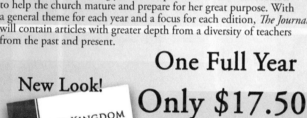